ONE POT, BIG POT

BY SHANE HETHERINGTON

13-Digit ISBN: 978-1-60433-807-2
10-Digit ISBN: 1-60433-807-5

This book may be ordered by mail from the publisher. Please include $5.99 for postage and handling. Please support your local bookseller first!

Books published by Cider Mill Press Book Publishers are available at special discounts for bulk purchases in the United States by corporations, institutions, and other organizations. For more information, please contact the publisher.

Cider Mill Press Book Publishers
"Where good books are ready for press"
PO Box 454
12 Spring Street
Kennebunkport, Maine 04046
Visit us online! www.cidermillpress.com

Typography: Archer
Image Credits: Page 85 by Johnny Hoell. Pages 5, 69, 73, 81, 82, 89, 131, 136, 143, 144, 148, 155, and 216 courtesy of Shutterstock. All other photos by Shane Hetherington.

Printed in China
1 2 3 4 5 6 7 8 9 0
First Edition

ONE POT
BIG POT

100 Family Meals Using One Cooking Vessel!

SHANE HETHERINGTON

CIDER MILL PRESS

BOOK PUBLISHERS

KENNEBUNKPORT, MAINE

CONTENTS

INTRODUCTION

I was not born a chef, and it did not come easy, but I always stuck by the lesson I learned while watching *Yan Can Cook* on PBS as a child: if Yan could do it, so could I. That show made me pick up a knife and get to work, and since then I've slowly but surely built my repertoire of dishes to where I can hold my own in any kitchen.

The key was soaking up all of the flavors around me. I moved around a lot while growing up, which I now see as a bit of good fortune since it exposed me to all sorts of different cuisines. Eventually, I fell in love with the flavors of Mexican and Southwestern cooking, and spent my teenage years and early 20s gobbling up everything Bobby Flay offered on the Food Network. As my own cooking has matured over the last half-decade, I have turned to chefs like Sean Brock, Virgilio Martínez Véliz, and Enrique Olvera for inspiration. Their respect for the food they prepare is what I aspire to in my cooking.

Writing this book brought me back to cooking with my dad. A seemingly always-tight budget forced us to get creative with whatever was kicking around in the cabinets, which, luckily, was what we both loved about cooking. When you've got limitations in the kitchen you can really have some fun, a belief upheld by this book's single-vessel restriction.

While cooking and eating are fun, what follows often isn't. No one wants to wash a bunch of dishes or scrape the stove after an evening of bouncing between pots on every burner. And when your kitchen is small like mine, a huge mess is even less appealing. With that in mind, I set out to make every aspect of the cooking process—from preparation to cleanup—as enjoyable and easy as possible.

As someone whose own horizons were expanded by cooking, I believe that cookbooks should open doors for people instead of intimidate them. Working from this premise, I attempted to make some challenging dishes more approachable. Since every recipe is completed in one cooking vessel, everything gets a little simpler.

I feel confident that, whether you're cooking for the family or for yourself, every recipe in this book will lighten your load, allowing you to get back to what cooking should be all about: sharing what you've learned with your loved ones.

BREAKFAST

Nearly everyone says breakfast is the most important meal of the day, but very few people talk about how difficult it is to find the motivation to prep something worthwhile. This chapter is full of easy, delicious, wholesome recipes that will carry you through whatever comes your way. From classics like the Bananas Foster French Toast (see page 4) and Huevos Rancheros (see page 11) to new favorites like Cashew Milk and Mung Bean Porridge with Black Vinegar (see page 24) and Chia Seed Pudding with Baker's Chocolate and Cherries (see page 27), we've got no shortage of dishes that will wipe every last bit of sleep from your eyes.

BANANAS FOSTER FRENCH TOAST

YIELD: *4 TO 6 SERVINGS*	**ACTIVE TIME:** *10 MINUTES*	**START TO FINISH:** *10 MINUTES*

The ultimate combination of decadent breakfast and sweet boozy dessert, this combination of Bananas Foster and classic French toast is something that is sure to win over everyone.

FRENCH TOAST

3 TABLESPOONS BUTTER

8 EGGS

2 TABLESPOONS SUGAR

½ CUP HEAVY CREAM

1 TABLESPOON CINNAMON

1 TABLESPOON VANILLA
    EXTRACT

PINCH OF SALT

1 LOAF BRIOCHE, CUT INTO 10
    TO 12 SLICES

BANANAS FOSTER

1 STICK BUTTER

½ CUP LIGHT BROWN SUGAR,
    PACKED

3 BANANAS, CUT LENGTHWISE
    AND HALVED

¼ CUP DARK RUM

½ CUP HEAVY CREAM

POWDERED SUGAR, FOR TOPPING

FRENCH TOAST

Preheat the oven to 200°F. Heat a large nonstick skillet over medium-high heat and melt 1 tablespoon of butter per batch of French toast.

In a bowl, add the eggs, sugar, heavy cream, cinnamon, vanilla, and salt and stir to combine. Dunk the slices of bread in the batter to cover both sides. Cook the bread in batches for 1 minute per side, or until a slight brown crust forms. Remove from the pan and keep warm in the oven.

BANANAS FOSTER

Place the skillet over medium-high heat. Add the stick of butter and the brown sugar.

Once the butter and sugar are melted, add the bananas to the pan and cook for 3 minutes. Shake the pan and use a spoon to cover the bananas with the sauce.

Pull the pan away from the heat and add the rum. Using a long match or a lighter, carefully light the rum on fire. Place the pan back on the heat and shake the pan until the flames are gone.

Add the remaining ½ cup of cream. Stir to blend and pour over the French toast. Sprinkle with powdered sugar and serve.

Tip: When adding alcohol to hot pans, make sure you pull them away from heat before adding the alcohol. This will help you avoid potential fires and injuries.

BLUEBERRY BREAD PUDDING

YIELD: *4 TO 6 SERVINGS*	**ACTIVE TIME:** *10 MINUTES*	**START TO FINISH:** *1 HOUR*

On the New England seacoast, Maine blueberries are everywhere. They are incredibly delicious, and discovering new ways to use them is a lot of fun. This recipe is also a perfect way to use up stale bread.

½ CUP SUGAR

3 EGGS

1 TABLESPOON VANILLA EXTRACT

1 CUP HALF-AND-HALF

1 TEASPOON SALT

2 CUPS BLUEBERRIES

1 BAGUETTE, CUT INTO CUBES

GREEK YOGURT, FOR TOPPING
  (OPTIONAL)

WHIPPED CREAM, FOR TOPPING
  (OPTIONAL)

Preheat oven to 350°F.

In a mixing bowl, mix all the ingredients together except for the blueberries and bread. Once combined, add the blueberries and bread.

Grease a glass 9 x 13-inch baking dish. Pour the mixture into the baking dish and put it in the oven. Cook for 50 to 60 minutes, or until a knife inserted into the center of the pudding comes out dry.

If desired, top with Greek yogurt or whipped cream and serve.

LAMB AND SWEET POTATO HASH

YIELD: *4 TO 6 SERVINGS*	**ACTIVE TIME:** *20 MINUTES*	**START TO FINISH:** *13 TO 17 HOURS*

This is something I came up with when I was working in a big dining hall that served breakfast, lunch, and dinner. After a big Easter meal, the chef at the time asked me to think of a breakfast that could utilize all of the leftover leg of lamb. If you really want to take this dish to the next level, fry an egg and place it on top.

MARINADE

4 GARLIC CLOVES, PUREED

3 SPRIGS OF OREGANO, MINCED

¼ CUP DIJON MUSTARD

¼ CUP CABERNET SAUVIGNON

1 TABLESPOON KOSHER SALT

1 TABLESPOON CRACKED BLACK PEPPER

LAMB & SWEET POTATO HASH

1½ POUNDS LEG OF LAMB, BUTTERFLIED

4 TABLESPOONS BEEF TALLOW OR CLARIFIED BUTTER

2 CUPS WATER

1 POUND SWEET POTATOES, PEELED AND MINCED

2 POBLANO PEPPERS, DICED (IF YOU WANT A LITTLE MORE HEAT, SUBSTITUTE 1 LARGE JALAPEÑO FOR ONE OF THE POBLANOS)

2 MEDIUM YELLOW ONIONS, MINCED

1 TABLESPOON GARLIC, MINCED

1 TABLESPOON CUMIN

1 TABLESPOON KOSHER SALT, PLUS MORE FOR SEASONING

1 TABLESPOON FRESH OREGANO, CHOPPED

BLACK PEPPER TO TASTE

MARINADE

Combine all of the ingredients for the marinade in a small bowl, then transfer to a 1-gallon freezer bag. Place the lamb in the bag, squeeze all of the air out, and place in the refrigerator for 12 to 16 hours.

LAMB & SWEET POTATO HASH

Preheat oven to 350°F. Place a cast-iron skillet over medium-high heat and add half of the beef tallow or clarified butter. Remove the lamb from the bag, place in the skillet, and sear for 5 minutes on each side.

Add 2 cups of water to the skillet, place it in the oven, and cook for 20 minutes, or until the center of the lamb reaches 140°F. Remove the skillet from the oven, set the lamb aside, and drain the liquid from the skillet. Let the lamb sit for 15 minutes and then mince.

Fill the skillet with water and bring to a boil. Add the sweet potatoes and cook for about 5 minutes, until they are just tender. Be careful not to overcook them, as you don't want to end up with mashed potatoes. Drain potatoes and set aside.

Add the remaining beef tallow or clarified butter, the poblano peppers, onions, garlic, and cumin to the skillet and cook over medium heat until all of the vegetables are soft, about 10 minutes.

Return the potatoes and the lamb to the skillet. Add the salt and cook for another 15 minutes. Add the oregano at the very end, season with black pepper, and serve.

Tip: Some stores will have butterflied legs of lamb ready to go. If not, you can always ask your butcher to butterfly it for you. Or, if you're feeling a bit adventurous, you can do it yourself.

HUEVOS RANCHEROS

YIELD: *6 SERVINGS*	**ACTIVE TIME:** *10 MINUTES*	**START TO FINISH:** *20 MINUTES*

*This classic, super-simple Mexican dish is
one of my go-to choices for brunch.*

3 TABLESPOONS COOKING OIL OR
   BEEF TALLOW

1 RED BELL PEPPER, DICED

2 ANAHEIM PEPPERS, SEEDED AND
   DICED

½ CUP RED ONION, DICED

1½ CUPS TOMATOES, DICED

1½ POUNDS BLACK BEANS,
   COOKED

¼ CUP CILANTRO, CHOPPED

1 TABLESPOON CUMIN

1 TABLESPOON KOSHER SALT

1 TABLESPOON BLACK PEPPER

12 EGGS

CORN TORTILLAS, WARMED

LIME WEDGES, FOR GARNISH
   (OPTIONAL)

Preheat oven to 350°F.

Heat the oil or tallow in a large cast-iron skillet over medium-high heat. Add the peppers and onion and sauté until softened.

Add the tomatoes and cook for 1 minute. Then, stir in the cooked black beans, cilantro, and cumin. Add the salt and pepper and cook for 2 minutes.

Make 12 small holes in the bean mixture for the eggs. Crack the eggs into the open spots. Put the skillet into the oven and cook until the whites are set, about 5 minutes.

Serve with warm tortillas and, if desired, lime wedges.

Tip: If you don't want to cook the black beans ahead of time, you can use canned. Just make sure to drain the liquid off before adding them to the skillet.

BREAKFAST TACOS

YIELD: *6 SERVINGS*	**ACTIVE TIME:** *10 TO 40 MINUTES*	**START TO FINISH:** *70 TO 100 MINUTES*

Tacos are the best thing ever, and any time you can start your day off with them is a double win. The add-ons are what make this the ultimate post-party breakfast, since everyone can tailor the tacos to their liking.

TACOS

2 TABLESPOONS COOKING OIL

8 EGGS

1 TABLESPOON CHILI POWDER

1 TABLESPOON CUMIN

½ TABLESPOON ADOBO SEASONING

1 TABLESPOON DRIED OREGANO

2 TABLESPOONS CILANTRO, CHOPPED

6 CORN TORTILLAS, WARMED

PICO DE GALLO

4 ROMA OR PLUM TOMATOES, DICED

1 JALAPEÑO PEPPER, DICED

½ CUP RED ONION

¼ CUP CILANTRO, CHOPPED

ZEST AND JUICE OF ½ A LIME

SALT TO TASTE

GUACAMOLE

2 RIPE AVOCADOES, SMASHED

2 TABLESPOONS CILANTRO, CHOPPED

2 TABLESPOONS RED ONION, MINCED

ZEST AND JUICE OF ½ A LIME

1 TABLESPOON JALAPEÑO PEPPER,
        MINCED (OPTIONAL)

SALT TO TASTE

TACOS

Heat the oil in a cast-iron skillet over medium heat. In a separate bowl, mix together the eggs, spices, and cilantro.

Add the egg mixture to the skillet and scramble until eggs are cooked through.

Serve with warm tortillas, Pico de Gallo, Guacamole, and other fixings of your choice.

PICO DE GALLO

Combine all ingredients in a bowl. Refrigerate for up to 1 hour before serving to let the flavors mingle.

GUACAMOLE

Mash all of the ingredients together in a small bowl and set aside.

Tip: Some other great toppings for these tacos are hot sauce, Cotija or goat cheese, shredded cheddar, and fresh cilantro. Feel free to add your own favorites to the mix.

BAKED EGG CASSEROLE WITH SPINACH, TOMATO, SCALLIONS, AND SHAVED PARMESAN

YIELD: *6 SERVINGS*	**ACTIVE TIME:** *15 MINUTES*	**START TO FINISH:** *60 TO 70 MINUTES*

This dish involves little work but is a great alternative to plain scrambled eggs. If you are serving this for brunch, try whipping up an arugula salad with a little truffle oil, shaved Parmesan, and fresh cracked pepper.

12 LARGE EGGS

¼ CUP WATER

½ CUP HALF-AND-HALF

3 PLUM TOMATOES, QUARTERED AND SLICED INTO WEDGES

1 CUP SPINACH, ROUGHLY CHOPPED

½ CUP SCALLIONS, CHOPPED

1 CUP PARMESAN CHEESE, GRATED, PLUS MORE FOR TOPPING

1 TABLESPOON FRESH THYME, CHOPPED

SALT AND PEPPER TO TASTE

Preheat oven to 350°F.

In a mixing bowl, scramble the eggs with the water and half-and-half.

Place all of the other ingredients, save the salt and pepper, in the mixing bowl and stir to combine. Pour the mixture into a greased 8 x 8-inch baking pan.

Season with salt and pepper. Put in the oven for 1 hour, or until the eggs are set in the middle.

Remove the pan from the oven and let the casserole stand for 5 minutes before serving. Grate additional Parmesan onto the top and serve.

Tip: To test whether the eggs are cooked, insert a knife into the dish. If it comes out dry, the eggs are ready.

HONEY-BAKED HAM, SWISS, AND SPINACH QUICHE

YIELD: *6 TO 8 SERVINGS*	**ACTIVE TIME:** *10 MINUTES*	**START TO FINISH:** *60 TO 70 MINUTES*

This simple recipe is great for a small Sunday brunch. It is easy to make, easy to clean up, and filling enough that you won't be hungry 2 hours later: exactly what you want on a Sunday.

1 READY-MADE PIECRUST

8 EGGS

1½ CUPS LIGHT CREAM

SALT AND PEPPER TO TASTE

PINCH OF FRESH NUTMEG, GROUND

1 CUP BABY SPINACH

5 OZ. SWISS CHEESE

½ POUND HONEY-BAKED HAM, DICED

Preheat the oven to 375°F.

Grease a 9-inch pie pan with nonstick cooking spray. Roll the piecrust into the pan, pressing down so that there are no bubbles.

Whisk together the eggs, cream, and seasonings until the mixture is smooth.

Layer the pan with the spinach, Swiss cheese, and ham. Then, cover the ingredients with the egg mixture and bake in the oven for 45 to 55 minutes, or until the eggs are set.

Remove the pan from the oven. Let the quiche rest for 5 minutes, cut into wedges, and serve.

PEANUT BUTTER AND BACON OATS WITH FRIED EGGS

YIELD: *4 TO 6 SERVINGS*	ACTIVE TIME: *5 MINUTES*	START TO FINISH: *10 TO 20 MINUTES*

Peanut butter, bacon, and eggs in oats? I know, it sounds crazy at first, but the saltiness of the crispy bacon, the nutty texture of the peanut butter, and the creaminess of the egg yolk work really well together, for a brand-new take on oatmeal.

6 SLICES THICK-CUT BACON

6 EGGS

2 CUPS OATS

6 CUPS WATER

1 TABLESPOON KOSHER SALT

¼ CUP PEANUT BUTTER OF YOUR CHOICE (I PREFER NATURAL CHUNKY PEANUT BUTTER)

Cook the bacon in a cast-iron skillet over medium heat. Remove the bacon from the skillet and use the bacon fat to fry the eggs.

Once the eggs are fried, remove them from the skillet and set aside. Wipe the remaining grease from the skillet with a paper towel. Add oats, water, and salt and cook for 7 to 10 minutes over medium heat, or until the oats are the desired consistency.

While the oats are cooking, chop the bacon. Add the bacon and peanut butter to the oatmeal. Stir to combine.

Top each portion with a fried egg and serve.

OVERNIGHT POMEGRANATE FREEKEH AND OATS

YIELD: *4 TO 6 SERVINGS*	ACTIVE TIME: *5 MINUTES*	START TO FINISH: *2 DAYS*

The recent craze for overnight oats got me thinking about using other grains and seeds to make a nutrient- and flavor-packed breakfast. Freekeh is delicious and full of protein. Pair it with Greek yogurt and you have a protein-rich breakfast with minimal cleanup.

1 CUP FREEKEH

1 CUP OATS

2 CUPS POMEGRANATE JUICE

½ CUP UNSWEETENED ALMOND MILK

½ CUP NONFAT GREEK YOGURT

¼ CUP FLAXSEED

3 TABLESPOONS HONEY

½ TEASPOON KOSHER SALT

Mix all of the ingredients together in a jar and place in the refrigerator.

After the first day, stir and put back in refrigerator for 1 more day.

Tip: Pack in 1-cup containers for a quick, on-the-go breakfast.

CREAMY SWEET POTATO LENTILS

YIELD: *6 SERVINGS*	**ACTIVE TIME:** *20 MINUTES*	**START TO FINISH:** *45 MINUTES*

Why should oatmeal get to hog the morning spotlight? Lentils are packed with fiber and protein, so you can get a complete meal in one shot.

1 POUND BROWN LENTILS, RINSED AND DRAINED

3 SMALL SWEET POTATOES, PEELED AND DICED

¾ CUP LIGHT CREAM OR HALF-AND-HALF

3¼ CUPS UNSWEETENED ALMOND MILK

4 CUPS UNSWEETENED CASHEW MILK

¼ CUP MAPLE SYRUP

1 TABLESPOON VANILLA EXTRACT

1 TEASPOON ALLSPICE

ZEST OF 1 ORANGE

PINCH OF SALT

CASHEWS, CRUSHED, FOR GARNISH

ALMONDS, CRUSHED, FOR GARNISH

Place all ingredients in an electric pressure cooker, seal the lid, and turn it on. It should take about 17 to 22 minutes for the cooker to seal and the lid to lock, so make sure to factor this into your cooking time.

Cook for 20 minutes, then carefully release the steam for about 2 minutes.

Remove the lid and garnish with the crushed cashews and almonds.

Tip: If you don't have a pressure cooker, use a crock-pot and cook on low for 8 hours, or until the lentils and sweet potatoes become smooth.

CASHEW MILK AND MUNG BEAN PORRIDGE WITH INFUSED BLACK VINEGAR

YIELD: *6 SERVINGS*	ACTIVE TIME: *15 MINUTES*	START TO FINISH: *5 HOURS AND 30 MINUTES*

This twist on a traditional Indonesian breakfast replaces the water with cashew milk for a richer, creamier result. The red plum-infused black vinegar adds both sweet and sour notes.

1 CUP MUNG BEANS, WASHED

5 CUPS CASHEW MILK, PLUS MORE
AS NEEDED

1 CINNAMON STICK

1 (3-INCH) PIECE OF GINGER,
PEELED AND CRUSHED

1 CUP LIGHT BROWN SUGAR

PINCH OF SALT

½ CUP WHITE RICE

BLACK VINEGAR INFUSED WITH
DRIED RED PLUMS

CASHEWS, CRUSHED, FOR
GARNISH

Place the mung beans, cashew milk, cinnamon stick, ginger, brown sugar, and salt in a crock-pot. Cover and cook on high for 4½ hours.

Add the rice, reduce heat to low, and cook until soft, about 1 hour. If the porridge starts to look dry, stir in an additional cup of cashew milk.

Discard the cinnamon stick and the ginger. Ladle the porridge into bowls and add more cashew milk if needed. Drizzle infused vinegar on top, garnish with cashews, and serve.

Tips: Dried red plums and black vinegar are specialty items that you might have to order online if you do not live near an Asian specialty market.

To infuse vinegar, place 1 to 2 cups of black vinegar and 6 to 8 dried red plums in a jar with a tight-fitting lid. Place in the cabinet for a minimum of 2 days.

For a quicker infusion process, place 3 cups of black vinegar and 6 to 8 dried red plums in a small saucepan and cook over the lowest available heat setting until the vinegar has reduced by ⅓. Transfer to the refrigerator and chill for 2 to 3 hours.

CHIA SEED PUDDING WITH BAKER'S CHOCOLATE AND CHERRIES

YIELD: *4 SERVINGS*	**ACTIVE TIME:** *5 TO 10 MINUTES*	**START TO FINISH:** *12 HOURS*

This has been my go-to quick breakfast as of late. It is easy to make and lasts for a few days in your refrigerator, if you haven't eaten it all by then.

1½ CUPS LITE COCONUT MILK

½ CUP NONFAT GREEK YOGURT

1 CUP SWEET DARK CHERRIES, FRESH OR FROZEN

½ CUP CHIA SEEDS

1 OZ. BAKER'S UNSWEETENED CHOCOLATE

2 TABLESPOONS HONEY

PINCH OF SALT

Add all ingredients to a blender and blend until it reaches the desired consistency.

Let the pudding set up in the refrigerator overnight to give the chia seeds time to soften and let all of the flavors meld together.

Tip: Baker's Unsweetened Chocolate is 100% cocoa with no dairy or sugar added. If you are looking for a slightly sweeter version of this pudding, try using a chocolate with between 85% to 95% cocoa content.

PEANUT BUTTER AND BANANA YOGURT BOWL WITH CHIA SEEDS

YIELD: *4 SERVINGS*	ACTIVE TIME: *10 MINUTES*	START TO FINISH: *10 MINUTES*

Super quick, super delicious, and super nutritious.
In other words, this a super way to start your day.

4 CUPS NONFAT GREEK YOGURT

½ CUP UNSALTED PEANUT BUTTER

3 BANANAS

3 TABLESPOONS CHIA SEEDS,
    PLUS 4 TABLESPOONS FOR
    GARNISH

4 CUPS BABY SPINACH

4 TABLESPOONS UNSWEETENED
    COCONUT FLAKES, FOR
    GARNISH

4 TABLESPOONS PEANUTS,
    CRUSHED, FOR GARNISH

Place all of the ingredients, besides the garnishes, in a food processor. Puree until smooth.

Top with the garnishes and serve.

Tip: If you cannot eat peanuts, you can use almond or cashew butter as a substitute.

SALADS

This chapter attempts to solve the age-old debate: Do I want something quick, or do I need something a bit more satisfying? The salads in here are light and easy, but freighted with enough flavor to keep you from feeling hungry when you walk away from the table. There are options here to answer almost any hankering. Need some protein? Try the Sofrito and Quinoa Salad with Pumpkin Seeds (see page 44). Yearning for the fruits of the sea? Whip up the Thai Chili, Shrimp, and Basil Salad (see page 36) or the Greek Couscous and Shrimp Salad (see page 39). Once you spend a little time with the recipes here, you're certain to stop viewing the salad as a last resort.

CURRIED CHICKEN SALAD WITH APPLES AND PECANS

YIELD: *6 SERVINGS*	**ACTIVE TIME:** *15 TO 20 MINUTES*	**START TO FINISH:** *45 MINUTES*

Madras curry powder provides a layer of flavor that goes well with the tart Granny Smith apples and the rich pecans. Serve over a bed of peppery baby arugula or between slices of toasted marble rye.

1½ POUNDS BONELESS, SKINLESS CHICKEN BREASTS, CUT INTO ½-INCH THICK CUTLETS

SALT AND PEPPER, TO TASTE

DASH OF OLIVE OIL

1 CUP MAYONNAISE

3 TABLESPOONS FRESH LIME JUICE

¼ CUP MADRAS CURRY POWDER

1 TABLESPOON CUMIN

1 TABLESPOON GRANULATED GARLIC

½ TEASPOON CINNAMON

½ TEASPOON TURMERIC

2 CUPS CELERY, MINCED

2 GRANNY SMITH APPLES, MINCED

½ RED BELL PEPPER, SEEDED AND MINCED

½ CUP PECANS, PLUS ¼ CUP FOR GARNISH, CHOPPED

5 TO 6 OZ. BABY ARUGULA (OPTIONAL)

SLICES OF MARBLE RYE (OPTIONAL)

Preheat oven to 350°F.

Place the chicken on a baking sheet. Season with salt and pepper and drizzle with enough olive oil to coat. Place the chicken in the oven and bake for 30 minutes, or until the center of the chicken reaches 160°F. Remove from the oven and let rest for 10 minutes so that the chicken cools and retains its juices.

In a large salad bowl, mix the mayonnaise, lime juice, and all of the spices together. Add the celery, apples, red pepper, and the pecans and stir.

Once the chicken is cool, dice into small cubes and add to the bowl. Add the arugula and toss to combine.

Serve over a bed of arugula or make into a sandwich with pieces of toasted marble rye. Garnish with additional pecans and serve.

TOASTED WHEAT BERRY SALAD WITH AVOCADO AND LIME YOGURT DRESSING

YIELD: *1 TO 2 SERVINGS*	**ACTIVE TIME:** *30 MINUTES*	**START TO FINISH:** *3 TO 24 HOURS*

Don't hesitate to tinker with this one. If you don't like spinach, you can use baby arugula to give the salad a nice peppery bite. Or, instead of the pickled onions, you could add some pickled jalapeños and give it a little kick.

PICKLED ONIONS

1½ CUPS RED ONIONS, SLICED
   THIN

1 TABLESPOON KOSHER SALT

1 TABLESPOON RAW APPLE CIDER
   VINEGAR

AVOCADO AND LIME YOGURT DRESSING

½ OF AN AVOCADO

1 CUP NONFAT GREEK YOGURT

ZEST AND JUICE OF 1 LIME

PINCH OF CAYENNE PEPPER

1 TABLESPOON CILANTRO

Continued...

PICKLED ONIONS

Place the onions in a mixing bowl with the salt and apple cider vinegar. Mash by hand until soft enough to fit into a ½-cup measuring cup. Place onions in a bowl. Bring 2 cups of water to boil and pour over the onions. Cover the bowl with plastic wrap and let sit for 30 minutes. Remove the plastic wrap and cool in the refrigerator until the rest of the salad is ready. For added flavor, let chill for 24 hours before using.

AVOCADO AND LIME YOGURT DRESSING

Place all of the ingredients into a blender and puree until smooth. Transfer to a container and set aside.

Continued...

SALAD

½ CUP WHEAT BERRIES

1½ CUPS STOCK OF CHOICE

COCONUT OIL COOKING SPRAY

2 TABLESPOONS PUMPKIN SEEDS

1 TABLESPOON CURRY POWDER

COCONUT OIL COOKING SPRAY

1½ CUPS BABY SPINACH

½ CUP KALE SPROUTS

6 OZ. ROASTED CHICKEN BREAST OR
TOFU, DICED

1 ROASTED RED PEPPER, DICED

1 SMALL TOMATO, CUT INTO WEDGES

8 TO 12 ENGLISH CUCUMBERS,
SLICED THIN

1 TABLESPOON CILANTRO LEAVES

1 TABLESPOON PARSLEY LEAVES

SALAD

Preheat the oven to 350°F. Place the wheat berries on a baking sheet and bake in the oven for 10 to 15 minutes, or until you notice a nutty aroma. This will add another layer of flavor to the salad. Remove the wheat berries from the oven and add them to a saucepan with the stock.

Bring to a boil, then reduce to a simmer. Cover the pot and cook for 1 to 1½ hours, or until the wheat berries are al dente. Be careful not to overcook or they will become mushy. When done, they should still be slightly firm. Set the wheat berries aside to cool.

While the wheat berries are cooling, grease a baking sheet with the coconut oil cooking spray. Place the pumpkin seeds on the sheet and sprinkle with the curry powder. Place the tray in the oven and cook for 10 to 15 minutes, until the seeds are golden brown. Remove, transfer to a bowl, and set aside to cool.

When the wheat berries and pumpkin seeds have cooled, place the remaining ingredients in a mixing bowl. Add the wheat berries and pumpkin seeds and toss until combined. Top with Pickled Onions and serve with the Avocado and Lime Yogurt Dressing on the side.

Tip: To roast the pepper, place on a baking sheet and cook in the oven at 350°F for 20 to 30 minutes, or until the skin is charred.

THAI CHILI, SHRIMP, AND BASIL SALAD

YIELD: *6 SERVINGS*	ACTIVE TIME: *30 MINUTES*	START TO FINISH: *45 MINUTES*

This dish is perfect for anyone who loves spicy food, as the dressing adds significant heat thanks to the Sambal Oelek and Thai bird chilies.

DRESSING

2 RED THAI CHILIES

½ CUP SOY SAUCE

½ CUP SAMBAL OELEK

JUICE FROM 3 LIMES

¼ CUP BROWN SUGAR

1 TABLESPOON FRESH GINGER, PEELED

2 TABLESPOONS CURRY POWDER

SALAD

½ HEAD OF NAPA CABBAGE, CHOPPED

1 CUP MINT LEAVES, CHOPPED

2 CUPS BASIL LEAVES, CHOPPED

1 CUP CILANTRO WITH STEMS, DICED

1 RED ONION, SLICED THIN

3 SCALLIONS, SLICED THIN

1 CARROT, PEELED AND SLICED THIN ON A BIAS

1 POUND SHRIMP (16/20 PREFERRED), COOKED, PEELED, AND CUT INTO LARGE PIECES

¼ CUP RAW CASHEWS, CRUSHED, FOR GARNISH

DRESSING

Combine all of the dressing ingredients in a blender and puree until smooth.

SALAD

Place all of the salad ingredients in a mixing bowl and stir to combine.

Toss with the dressing and top with crushed cashews.

If you've got time and you want even more flavor, prepare the salad the day before and reserve ½ of the dressing for the second day. Serve the reserved dressing on the side or pour it on top.

Tip: The number in the parentheses beside the shrimp is an indication of their size, detailing how many you will get per pound.

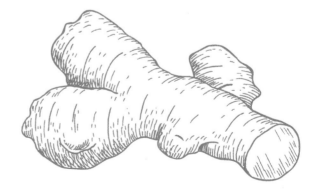

GREEK COUSCOUS AND SHRIMP SALAD

YIELD: *6 SERVINGS*	ACTIVE TIME: *40 MINUTES*	START TO FINISH: *50 MINUTES*

This light, shrimp-packed salad will have you going back for seconds.

SHRIMP

¾ POUND SHRIMP (16/20, SHELL ON PREFERRED)

6 BUNCHES OF MINT

10 GARLIC CLOVES, PEELED

SALAD

3½ CUPS CHICKEN STOCK

3 CUPS TOASTED ISRAELI COUSCOUS

1 BUNCH OF ASPARAGUS, BOTTOM 2 INCHES REMOVED

3 ROMA TOMATOES, DICED

2 TABLESPOONS MINT, CHOPPED

1 TABLESPOON OREGANO, CHOPPED

½ ENGLISH CUCUMBER, DICED

ZEST AND JUICE OF 1 LARGE LEMON

½ CUP RED ONION, DICED

½ CUP SUN-DRIED TOMATOES, SLICED THIN

¼ CUP PITTED KALAMATA OLIVES, CHOPPED

⅓ CUP GREEK OLIVE OIL OR EXTRA VIRGIN OLIVE OIL

½ CUP FETA CHEESE CRUMBLES

SALT AND PEPPER TO TASTE

SHRIMP

Place the shrimp, mint, and garlic in a stockpot and cover with water. Cook over medium heat until shrimp are cooked through. The shrimp should be firm and pink when done. Remove the shrimp from the pot, chill in the refrigerator, peel, and cut in half lengthwise. Set aside.

SALAD

In a large stockpot, bring chicken stock to a boil and add the couscous. Reduce the heat to a simmer. Cover and cook for 7 to 10 minutes. Strain and chill the couscous immediately to avoid overcooking.

Fill the pot back up with water and bring to a boil. Add the asparagus and cook for 1 to 1½ minutes until it has softened a bit. Quickly strain in a colander and cover with ice cubes to stop the cooking process. This will keep the asparagus green and firm. Chop the asparagus into bite-sized pieces.

Add all the remaining ingredients, besides the feta, to a salad bowl. Add the couscous and asparagus and stir to combine. Top with the shrimp and the feta and serve.

Tip: You can buy couscous pre-toasted, but if you are looking to bring your dish to the next level, toast your couscous in the oven at 375°F for 10 to 12 minutes on a baking sheet. This will add a delightful nutty flavor to the dish.

QUINOA AND BLACK BEAN SALAD

YIELD: *4 TO 6 SERVINGS*	ACTIVE TIME: *25 MINUTES*	START TO FINISH: *24 HOURS*

I have always loved quinoa and Southwestern flavors, so combining the two was a no-brainer. Packed with protein, this is a guilt-free way to get a ton of nutrition.

1 POUND BLACK BEANS

1 CUP QUINOA

2 CUPS WATER OR STOCK OF CHOICE

1 CUP SALSA VERDE (SEE PAGE 193)

4 TOMATILLOS, RINSED AND DICED

2 FRESNO CHILIES, SLICED THIN (FOR LESS SPICE, REMOVE SEEDS BEFORE SLICING)

1 YELLOW BELL PEPPER, SEEDED AND DICED

1 CUP BABY SPINACH

1 TABLESPOON KOSHER SALT

1 TABLESPOON CUMIN

1 TABLESPOON GARLIC POWDER

1 TABLESPOON DRIED OREGANO

In a bowl, cover the beans with water and soak overnight.

Thoroughly wash the quinoa in a fine mesh strainer to remove the outer layer.

In a small saucepan with a lid, add the water or stock and bring to a boil. Add the quinoa. Reduce heat to low, cover, and cook for 15 minutes.

Remove lid and fluff with a fork, then transfer to a large salad bowl.

Drain and rinse the beans. Place them in the same saucepan used for the quinoa.

Cover with fresh water and cook over medium heat until the beans are fork tender but still have a little texture. Stir occasionally to keep the beans from sticking to the pan. Cook for about 70 minutes.

While the beans are cooking, add the remaining ingredients to the quinoa, stir to combine, and place the salad bowl in the refrigerator until the beans are done cooking.

Drain and rinse beans with cold water until cool. Add to salad bowl, stir to combine, and serve.

Tip: If you do not have time to soak beans overnight or you just want a quick fix, you can use the same amount of canned beans. Make sure to rinse the canned beans thoroughly before cooking, and use the low-sodium variety to maintain the salt balance in the recipe.

CITRUS AND QUINOA SALAD WITH DRIED CRANBERRIES AND WALNUTS

YIELD: *6 SERVINGS*	ACTIVE TIME: *30 MINUTES*	START TO FINISH: *45 MINUTES*

This salad works any time of year. Since quinoa is packed with protein, it's the perfect for those nights when you don't want something heavy.

SALAD

1½ CUPS QUINOA, WASHED

3 CUPS WATER

1 TEASPOON KOSHER SALT

½ POUND CARROTS, PEELED AND JULIENNED

1 MEDIUM SHALLOT, PEELED, HALVED LENGTHWISE, CUT INTO THIN HALF-MOONS

½ CUP DRIED CRANBERRIES

½ CUP WALNUTS, CRUSHED

ZEST AND SEGMENTS OF 2 BLOOD ORANGES (RESERVE THE MEMBRANES AND JUICE FOR THE DRESSING)

DRESSING

RESERVED MEMBRANES AND JUICE FROM 2 BLOOD ORANGES

JUICE OF 1 LIME

¼ CUP RICE VINEGAR

½ CUP CANOLA OIL (OR PREFERRED NEUTRAL OIL)

¼ CUP HONEY

1 TABLESPOON KOSHER SALT

SALAD

Add the quinoa, water, and salt to a medium saucepan and bring to a boil. Once the quinoa starts to boil, reduce the heat to medium or medium-low and simmer until the quinoa has absorbed all of the water. Remove the pan from heat and cover for 5 to 10 minutes. Remove the cover, fluff with a fork, and let cool.

Place the carrots, shallot, cranberries, walnuts, blood orange zest, blood orange segments, and the quinoa in a salad bowl and stir until combined. Serve with the dressing on the side.

DRESSING

Place the ingredients for the dressing in a blender and puree until smooth. Transfer to a container with a lid and set aside.

Tip: If you want the quinoa to cool as evenly as possible, line a baking sheet with parchment paper and pour the quinoa onto it in an even layer. Once it's cool, just fold up the paper and transfer the quinoa wherever you want it.

SOFRITO AND QUINOA SALAD WITH PUMPKIN SEEDS

YIELD: *4 TO 6 SERVINGS*	ACTIVE TIME: *15 MINUTES*	START TO FINISH: *4 HOURS AND 15 MINUTES*

This twist on traditional Spanish rice gives you the flavor you crave while adding protein in the form of quinoa and pumpkin seeds. You won't even think twice about going back for another scoop.

2 POBLANO PEPPERS, SEEDED

1 WHITE ONION, PEELED AND CUT INTO QUARTERS

1 RED BELL PEPPER, SEEDED

1 GREEN BELL PEPPER, SEEDED

3 PLUM TOMATOES

2 GARLIC CLOVES, PEELED

1 TABLESPOON CUMIN

2 TABLESPOONS ADOBO SEASONING

1½ CUPS QUINOA, WASHED

PUMPKIN SEEDS, TOASTED AND SALTED, FOR GARNISH

Dice 1 of the poblanos, ½ of the onion, and ½ each of the bell peppers. Place these and the remaining ingredients, besides the quinoa, in a blender or food processor and puree until smooth.

Add the puree and quinoa to a crock-pot and cook on low for 4 hours.

Garnish with the pumpkin seeds and serve.

Tips: The puree resulting from Step 1 is Sofrito, an essential sauce in Latin cuisine. It is used in the Puerto Rican Rice and Beans with Chicken (see page 157) and White Chicken Chili (see page 158).

You can purchase toasted pumpkin seeds at most stores, but if you want to make them yourself, toss raw pumpkin seeds with a little canola oil and salt and bake at 325°F for 40 to 45 minutes, or until crunchy.

RAW BEET SALAD WITH BLOOD ORANGE, JALAPEÑO, AND BRIE

YIELD: *4 TO 6 SERVINGS*	ACTIVE TIME: *30 TO 40 MINUTES*	START TO FINISH: *24 HOURS*

Earthy, sweet, spicy, creamy, and healthy, this salad is a guaranteed winner.

5 TO 7 RED BEETS, PEELED
AND SHREDDED, STEMS
AND GREENS RESERVED

1 JALAPEÑO PEPPER, MINCED
(REMOVE SEEDS IF
YOU DON'T WANT THE
EXTRA SPICE)

½ TEASPOON KOSHER SALT

ZEST, SEGMENTS, AND JUICE
OF 1 BLOOD ORANGE

3 TABLESPOONS EXTRA
VIRGIN OLIVE OIL

3 TABLESPOONS HONEY

1 TABLESPOON RICE
VINEGAR

2 POUNDS ARUGULA

½ POUND BRIE, SLICED

Place the beet greens and stems in a bowl of ice water to remove any dirt.

Place the shredded beets and the jalapeño in a salad bowl.

Remove the beet greens and stems from the ice water and dice the stems. Set the greens aside. Add the beet stems to the salad bowl. Add salt and stir.

Using a microplane, zest the blood orange, making sure to avoid the white pith.

Peel the orange and remove the fruit from the membranes. Add the fruit to the salad bowl. Squeeze the juice from the remnants of the orange into the bowl.

In a separate small bowl, whisk the oil, honey, and vinegar together and pour over the beet mixture.

Cover the salad bowl and refrigerate for at least 2 hours. For best results, leave in the refrigerator overnight.

Mix the beet greens with arugula and place them in the salad bowl. Top with the beet salad and the Brie and serve.

Tip: Beets, while super delicious, stain everything they touch. I always use gloves when dealing with them so my fingers don't turn, well, "beet red." Make sure that whatever bowl you grate the beets into is big enough to put a box grater inside. This will prevent the beets from spilling and staining everything. When cooking with beets, I use stainless steel or glass cookware.

CHILI-DUSTED CAULIFLOWER AND CHICKPEA SALAD

YIELD: *4 TO 6 SERVINGS*	**ACTIVE TIME:** *25 MINUTES*	**START TO FINISH:** *45 MINUTES*

Crunchy cauliflower, fluffy chickpeas, and a perfect balance of sweet and spicy make this salad grand enough to serve as the main event.

SALAD

½ POUND CHICKPEAS, COOKED

1 HEAD OR 1½ CUPS OF PURPLE CAULIFLOWER,
    CUT INTO BITE-SIZED PIECES

1 HEAD OR 1½ CUPS WHITE CAULIFLOWER,
    CUT INTO BITE-SIZED PIECES

3 GARLIC CLOVES, SLICED THIN

1 SHALLOT, PEELED AND SLICED INTO THIN RINGS

⅓ CUP CANOLA OIL (OR PREFERRED NEUTRAL OIL)

½ OF THE SPICE BLEND (SEE RECIPE)

½ TABLESPOON KOSHER SALT

DRESSING

2 SCALLIONS, SLICED THIN

2 RED FRESNO PEPPERS, SEEDED AND SLICED
    INTO THIN RINGS

3 TABLESPOONS GRANULATED SUGAR

¼ CUP RED WINE VINEGAR

½ OF SPICE BLEND (SEE RECIPE)

SPICE BLEND

1 TEASPOON DARK CHILI POWDER

1 TEASPOON CHIPOTLE PEPPER POWDER

1 TEASPOON BLACK PEPPER

1 TEASPOON ONION POWDER

1 TEASPOON GARLIC POWDER

½ TEASPOON PAPRIKA

1 TABLESPOON KOSHER SALT

SALAD

Preheat the oven to 400°F.

Place all of the ingredients in a mixing bowl and toss to coat with the oil. Place the mixture in a 9 x 13-inch baking pan. Place the pan in the oven and bake for 30 minutes, or until the cauliflower is slightly charred and still crunchy. Place the cauliflower-and-chickpea mixture and the remaining spice blend into a bowl. Add the dressing, toss to coat, and serve.

DRESSING

Place all of the ingredients in the mixing bowl and stir with a fork until the sugar is dissolved.

SPICE BLEND

Place all of the ingredients in a small bowl and stir to combine.

TABBOULEH SALAD

YIELD: *6 SERVINGS*	ACTIVE TIME: *30 MINUTES*	START TO FINISH: *2 HOURS AND 30 MINUTES*

This has been my favorite salad for the past few years. It's super healthy and you can serve it with any meal. I add two sunny-side up eggs for a quick and satisfying breakfast.

½ CUP BULGUR WHEAT

2 BUNCHES OF CURLY PARSLEY, ROUGHLY CHOPPED (ABOUT 4 TO 6 CUPS)

¼ CUP RED ONION, MINCED

1 ENGLISH CUCUMBER, DICED

1 PINT CHERRY OR GRAPE TOMATOES, QUARTERED

1½ TABLESPOONS GARLIC, MINCED

1 TABLESPOON KOSHER SALT

1 TABLESPOON CRACKED BLACK PEPPER

2 TEASPOONS GROUND ALLSPICE

JUICE OF 1 LEMON

½ CUP EXTRA VIRGIN OLIVE OIL

Rinse the bulgur wheat to remove the film. Place in a bowl. Boil 1 cup of water and pour over the bulgur. Wrap tightly with plastic and set aside for 30 minutes.

Meanwhile, wash parsley to remove any dirt and shake dry before cutting.

After 30 minutes, drain off any excess liquid from the bulgur wheat and add to a salad bowl.

Cut all remaining vegetables and add them to the salad bowl. Add the parsley and the remaining ingredients to the salad bowl and stir to combine.

Refrigerate for at least 2 hours before serving.

Tips: English cucumbers are preferable due to their thin skin and smaller seeds, but Persian cucumbers are also good for this recipe. Make sure to keep the size difference in mind. You need about 1½ Persian cucumbers for every 1 English cucumber.

Two hours is the bare minimum you should let this salad sit. Personally, I recommend at least 24 hours before serving.

RICE NOODLE SALAD
WITH PEANUT SAUCE

YIELD: *6 SERVINGS*	**ACTIVE TIME:** *40 MINUTES*	**START TO FINISH:** *40 MINUTES*

This salad is perfect for those hot summer nights when you're terrified of turning on the oven.

PEANUT SAUCE

JUICE OF 2 LIMES

2 TABLESPOONS FRESH GINGER, PEELED

1 GARLIC CLOVE

¼ CUP BROWN SUGAR

2 TO 3 TABLESPOONS FISH SAUCE

2 TABLESPOONS DARK SOY SAUCE

½ CUP PEANUT BUTTER

SALAD

1 POUND RICE STICK NOODLES (BANH PHO)

½ POUND CARROTS, PEELED AND
JULIENNED

1 RED PEPPER, SEEDED AND JULIENNED

1 RED FRESNO PEPPER, SEEDED AND
JULIENNED

1 TO 2 JALAPEÑO PEPPERS, SEEDED AND
JULIENNED

4 SCALLIONS, SLICED THIN ON A BIAS

⅔ CUP THAI BASIL (IF USING TRADITIONAL
BASIL, USE 1 CUP)

¼ CUP CILANTRO, WASHED AND CHOPPED

1 TO 2 TABLESPOONS FRESH MINT,
CHOPPED

PEANUTS, CRUSHED, FOR GARNISH

PEANUT SAUCE

Place the ingredients into a food processor and puree. Transfer the dressing to a refrigerator and chill.

SALAD

In a large stockpot, bring water to a boil and add the noodles. Cook while stirring for 3 minutes, or until the noodles are tender. Drain the noodles and rinse with cold water.

Place the noodles and the remaining ingredients, besides the peanuts, in a salad bowl. Stir to combine, add the peanut sauce, and toss to coat. Garnish with the crushed peanuts and serve.

Tip: If you want to bulk up this salad, try adding shrimp for additional protein.

FIVE-BEAN SALAD WITH GOOSEBERRY VINAIGRETTE

YIELD: *6 SERVINGS*	**ACTIVE TIME:** *30 MINUTES*	**START TO FINISH:** *2 DAYS*

Slow cooking the beans in chicken stock and cooling them overnight provides a lovely counter to the sweet and tangy dressing.

SALAD

¼ POUND KIDNEY BEANS, SOAKED OVERNIGHT

¼ POUND CANNELLINI BEANS, SOAKED OVERNIGHT

¼ POUND PINK BEANS, SOAKED OVERNIGHT

¼ POUND PINTO BEANS, SOAKED OVERNIGHT

¼ POUND WHOLE DRIED GREEN PEAS, SOAKED OVERNIGHT

4 TO 6 CUPS CHICKEN STOCK

2 TABLESPOONS GRANULATED GARLIC

2 BAY LEAVES

PINCH OF CRUSHED RED PEPPER FLAKES

3 TABLESPOONS KOSHER SALT

2 CUPS CELERY, MINCED

¼ CUP RED RADISHES, GRATED (ABOUT 2 LARGE RADISHES)

1½ CUPS PARSNIP, PEELED AND MINCED (ABOUT 1 MEDIUM PARSNIP)

½ CUP PARSLEY

1 CUP SCALLION GREENS

JUICE OF ½ A LEMON

VINAIGRETTE

3½ OZ. GOOSEBERRIES, WASHED

¼ CUP RED WINE VINEGAR

¼ CUP HONEY

½ CUP EXTRA VIRGIN OLIVE OIL

1 TABLESPOON KOSHER SALT

SALAD

Drain and rinse the beans and peas and transfer them to a crock-pot. Add the chicken stock, granulated garlic, bay leaves, red pepper flakes, and kosher salt and cook on low for 8 hours, or until the beans are tender. Turn off the slow cooker and let the beans rest until they come to room temperature. Place the beans in the refrigerator overnight.

VINAIGRETTE

Place all of the vinaigrette ingredients into a blender and puree until the consistency is silky. The dressing should be thick enough to coat a spoon. Set the dressing aside.

Place all of the remaining salad ingredients in a large salad bowl. Stir until combined.

Drain the beans. Place the beans in the salad bowl, add half of the dressing, and toss. Serve with the remaining dressing on the side.

Tips: I strongly recommend soaking and slow cooking the beans for this recipe, as it imparts a far more complex flavor than using canned beans.

I like to use the reserved cooking liquid from the beans to thicken soups, sauces, and stews.

CROCK-POT

A crock-pot is the busy foodie's best friend, since they can get a dish started in the morning and come home to a delicious meal. It's also ideal for the weekend, since it allows you to reduce your to-do list by one. If the memory of some gelatinous crock-pot mish-mash from your childhood has you a little wary, give Grandma's Beef Stew (see page 61) a try. I'm pretty sure it'll exercise those demons.

BEEF CHILI

| **YIELD:** *6 SERVINGS* | **ACTIVE TIME:** *30 MINUTES* | **START TO FINISH:** *6½ TO 8½ HOURS* |

There's something perfect about a bowl of chili during football season. This version is so good, it won't even matter if your team ends up losing.

1½ POUNDS GROUND BEEF (80% LEAN RECOMMENDED)

1 (14 OZ.) CAN PEELED SAN MARZANO TOMATOES

1 (14 OZ.) CAN CRUSHED SAN MARZANO TOMATOES

1 RED BELL PEPPER, DICED

1 LARGE WHITE ONION OR 2 SMALL YELLOW ONIONS, DICED; PLUS MORE FOR GARNISH (OPTIONAL)

3 TO 4 GARLIC CLOVES, MINCED

1 JALAPEÑO PEPPER, MINCED (OPTIONAL)

1 POUND PINK BEANS, SOAKED AND DRAINED

¼ CUP CILANTRO, CHOPPED, PLUS MORE FOR GARNISH (OPTIONAL)

¼ CUP HOT SAUCE ⅛ CUP DARK CHILI POWDER

1 TABLESPOON BLACK PEPPER

1 TABLESPOON KOSHER SALT

2 TABLESPOONS GRANULATED GARLIC

⅓ CUP CUMIN

1 TABLESPOON HOT MADRAS CURRY POWDER

1 TABLESPOON GRANULATED GARLIC

1 TABLESPOON DRIED OREGANO

CHEDDAR CHEESE, GRATED, FOR GARNISH (OPTIONAL)

In a large skillet, cook the ground beef over medium heat until it is browned. Drain off the fat and set aside.

Add all of the ingredients to a crock-pot and cook on low for 6 to 8 hours. Once cooked, crush the whole tomatoes to release their juices. The beans should be soft to the touch before serving.

Garnish with cheese, onion, and cilantro, if desired.

Tip: If you want to reduce the cooking time to about 4 to 5 hours, you can use canned beans. Make sure to rinse and drain the canning liquid to avoid adding any additional salt to the recipe.

GRANDMA'S BEEF STEW

YIELD: *4 TO 6 SERVINGS*	**ACTIVE TIME:** *25 MINUTES*	**START TO FINISH:** *6½ TO 8½ HOURS*

This recipe perfectly captures the beauty of the crock-pot: prepare it the night before, turn the crock-pot on low before leaving in the morning, and come home to a house that smells amazing and a meal that's ready to go.

1½ POUNDS STEWING BEEF

2 TABLESPOONS KOSHER SALT

1 TABLESPOON BLACK PEPPER

1 TABLESPOON GRANULATED
ONION

1 TABLESPOON GRANULATED
GARLIC

½ TABLESPOON DRIED OREGANO

1 TEASPOON CELERY SEED

PINCH OF CRUSHED RED PEPPER
FLAKES

2 TABLESPOONS FRESH THYME

2 BAY LEAVES

4 CUPS BEEF STOCK

3 GARLIC CLOVES, MINCED

3 CARROTS, DICED

2 LEEKS, WHITES ONLY, CHOPPED

1 MEDIUM YELLOW ONION,
CHOPPED

2 YELLOW POTATOES, CHOPPED

2 CELERY STALKS, CHOPPED

3 OZ. TOMATO PASTE

¼ CUP WORCESTERSHIRE SAUCE

1 TABLESPOON SOY SAUCE

¼ CUP FLOUR

Place all of the ingredients, besides the flour and 1 cup of the stock, in a crock-pot and stir to combine.

Place the flour and reserved stock in a bowl and stir until smooth. Add this mixture to the crock-pot and cover. Cook on low heat until the beef is tender and the potatoes are soft.

COFFEE AND BOURBON BRISKET WITH GOAT CHEESE AND BRUSSELS SPROUTS SLAW

YIELD: *6 SERVINGS*	ACTIVE TIME: *10 TO 15 MINUTES*	START TO FINISH: *24 HOURS*

You'll love this marriage of Texan and Southern BBQ, where the subtle bitterness of the coffee and the sweet notes of the bourbon work beautifully together.

BRISKET

1 YELLOW ONION, DICED

1 PEACH, PEELED AND MINCED

1 NECTARINE, PEELED AND MINCED

½ OZ. FRESH GINGER, PEELED AND MINCED

½ CUP DRY RUB (SEE RECIPE PAGE 64)

3½ POUNDS BRISKET, FLAT CUT

1 CUP WATER

COFFEE AND BOURBON BBQ SAUCE

2 CUPS COFFEE, BREWED

¼ CUP DARK BROWN SUGAR

¾ CUP BOURBON

3 TABLESPOONS MOLASSES

¼ CUP RAW APPLE CIDER VINEGAR

2 TABLESPOONS WORCESTERSHIRE SAUCE

¼ CUP KETCHUP

1 TABLESPOON GRANULATED GARLIC

½ TABLESPOON BLACK PEPPER, COARSELY GROUND

1 TABLESPOON TAPIOCA STARCH OR CORNSTARCH

Continued...

BRISKET

Place the onion, peach, nectarine, and ginger in the crock-pot. Apply the dry rub to the brisket and place the brisket on top of the mixture in the crock-pot. Place the crock-pot in the refrigerator overnight.

Put the crock-pot on low, cover, and let cook for 8 hours. Turn off and let the meat rest for 1 hour.

COFFEE AND BOURBON BBQ SAUCE

While the brisket is cooking, combine all the ingredients for the BBQ sauce in a small saucepan. Cook until the alcohol has evaporated and the mixture has been reduced by at least ¼. The sauce should be thick enough to coat a spoon.

If you would rather have the brisket marinate in the sauce, remove the brisket from the crock-pot after 6 hours and discard the onions, ginger, and fruit along with any liquid. Add all of the ingredients for the BBQ sauce to the crock-pot and cook on high for 1 hour. Then return the brisket to the crock-pot and cook on low for the remaining time.

Continued...

GOAT CHEESE AND BRUSSELS SPROUTS SLAW

1 CUP MILK

2 TABLESPOONS WHITE VINEGAR

¾ CUP MAYONNAISE

¼ CUP NONFAT GREEK YOGURT

1½ TABLESPOONS PASILLA PEPPER
SEEDS, GROUND

1 CUP GOAT CHEESE, CRUMBLED

1 TABLESPOON BLACK PEPPER,
COARSELY GROUND

PINCH OF KOSHER SALT

JUICE OF ½ A LIME

1 TABLESPOON THAI BASIL,
MINCED

2 POUNDS BRUSSELS SPROUTS,
SHAVED

¼ POUND PARSNIPS, PEELED AND
GRATED

DRY RUB

¼ CUP GROUND COFFEE

1 TEASPOON GROUND CORIANDER
SEED

2 TEASPOONS BLACK PEPPER

PINCH OF CRUSHED RED PEPPER
FLAKES

1 TEASPOON CUMIN

2 TEASPOONS GROUND YELLOW
MUSTARD SEEDS

2 TEASPOONS DARK CHILI
POWDER

1 TEASPOON PAPRIKA

3 OZ. KOSHER SALT

3 OZ. LIGHT BROWN SUGAR

GOAT CHEESE AND BRUSSELS SPROUTS SLAW

Place everything, besides the brussels sprouts and parsnips, in a large bowl and whisk until combined. Reserve half of the dressing for drizzling.

Add the Brussels sprouts and parsnips to the bowl and toss to coat.

Remove the brisket from the pot and use a sharp knife to cut it into ½-inch slices against the grain. Serve with the slaw.

DRY RUB

Add all of the ingredients to a mixing bowl and stir to combine. Transfer the mixture to a mason jar and store for up to 6 months.

Tip: Pasilla pepper seeds are found inside the dried pepper pods. To turn them into powder, grind them with a mortar and pestle or run them through a coffee grinder.

PHO WITH STRIP STEAK

YIELD: *4 TO 6 SERVINGS*	**ACTIVE TIME:** *15 MINUTES*	**START TO FINISH:** *4½ TO 8½ HOURS*

This is a fairly traditional pho, but the possible variations are almost endless. The broth freezes well, so if you don't want to make a huge batch, it's not an issue.

BROTH

8 CUPS BEEF STOCK OR BROTH

1 LARGE CINNAMON STICK

4 BAY LEAVES

6 STAR ANISE

2 TEASPOONS SEA SALT

2 TEASPOONS BLACK PEPPERCORNS
(FOR A LITTLE MORE FLAVOR,
SUBSTITUTE SZECHUAN
PEPPERCORNS FOR 1 OF THE
TEASPOONS)

2 TEASPOONS CORIANDER SEEDS

1 TEASPOON ALLSPICE BERRIES

1 TEASPOON FENNEL SEEDS

4 TABLESPOONS FRESH GINGER, PEELED
AND SMASHED

6 GARLIC CLOVES, PEELED AND
SMASHED

4 LEMONGRASS STALKS, CRACKED OPEN

1 WHITE ONION, PEELED AND CUT INTO
6 WEDGES

2 TABLESPOONS LIQUID AMINOS OR
DARK SOY SAUCE

2 TABLESPOONS RICE VINEGAR

2 TABLESPOONS FISH SAUCE

Continued...

BROTH

Place all of the ingredients for the broth in a crock-pot. Cover and cook on low for at least 4 hours. For a stronger broth, cook for 8 hours.

Strain the broth through a fine sieve. Discard the solids and return the broth to the slow cooker.

Continued...

NOODLES AND STRIP STEAK

8 OZ. DRIED CHINESE YELLOW
NOODLES

4 BABY BOK CHOY, WASHED AND
QUARTERED

12 TO 18 OZ. PRIME N.Y. STRIP
STEAK

1 TO 1½ CUPS BEAN SPROUTS
(OPTIONAL)

2 CHILI PEPPERS, SLICED
(OPTIONAL)

SRIRACHA OR OTHER HOT SAUCE
TO TASTE

LIME WEDGES (OPTIONAL)

CILANTRO, WASHED AND TORN
(OPTIONAL)

THAI BASIL LEAVES, CHOPPED
(OPTIONAL)

SCALLIONS, CHOPPED (OPTIONAL)

NOODLES AND STRIP STEAK

After straining the broth, add the noodles and bok choy, cover, and cook for approximately 30 minutes, until the noodles are tender and the bok choy is al dente.

Slice the steak into ¼-inch pieces. Ladle the broth, noodles, and baby bok choy into bowls and top with the steak. The broth will cook the steak to rare. If you prefer the steak to be cooked more, add to the crock-pot and cook in the broth for 2 to 3 minutes for medium-rare, 3 to 5 minutes for medium. Season with Sriracha. If desired, serve with lime wedges and top with preferred combination of the bean sprouts, chili peppers, cilantro, Thai basil, and scallions.

Tips: If you don't want to have to strain the broth, place the spices, garlic, and ginger in two large coffee filters. Tie the filters closed with kitchen twine and place in the broth. When the broth is finished cooking, remove the spice pouch and the lemongrass stalks and discard.

Feel free to use your preferred chili pepper, but I've found that serrano, jalapeño, or Fresno work the best in this preparation.

BOLOGNESE

YIELD: 6 SERVINGS	ACTIVE TIME: 15 MINUTES	START TO FINISH: 8½ TO 12½ HOURS

This meat sauce is earthy, sweet, and rich. In other words, it's got everything you'd want out of a pasta dish.

- 1 POUND GROUND BEEF (85% LEAN)
- 1 POUND GROUND VEAL
- 1 POUND GROUND PORK
- 1 CARROT, PEELED AND MINCED
- 1 ONION, PEELED AND MINCED
- 2 CELERY STALKS, WASHED AND MINCED
- 1 CUP HEAVY CREAM
- 1 (28 OZ.) CAN OF SAN MARZANO STEWED TOMATOES AND THE JUICE
- 5 GARLIC CLOVES, ROASTED AND MASHED; OR 3 FRESH GARLIC CLOVES, MINCED
- 1 CUP RED WINE (CABERNET SAUVIGNON OR SYRAH PREFERRED)
- 3 TABLESPOONS DRIED OREGANO
- 1 TABLESPOON FENNEL SEEDS
- 1 TABLESPOON GARLIC POWDER
- SALT AND PEPPER TO TASTE
- 1 POUND PASTA, COOKED ACCORDING TO MANUFACTURER'S INSTRUCTIONS

Place the meat in a large sauté pan and cook over medium-high heat until it is cooked through and the fat has been rendered. Use a wooden spoon to break the meat up as it cooks.

Drain the fat from the pan and add the carrot, onion, and celery. Cook for 5 minutes, or until the vegetables have softened.

Add the cream and cook until it has been absorbed by the meat and vegetables.

Crush the tomatoes in your hands. Add the contents of the sauté pan and the remaining ingredients to a crock-pot, season with salt and pepper, cover, and cook on low for 8 to 12 hours.

When the sauce has finished cooking, serve over cooked pasta.

Tips: If you want to cook the pasta with the sauce, add it to the crock-pot when the sauce has 30 minutes remaining in the crock-pot and check periodically to make sure the pasta does not overcook.

For a lighter sauce, substitute half-and-half or whole milk for the heavy cream.

PEPPERED PORK SHOULDER WITH APPLES, CARROTS, AND ONIONS

YIELD: *4 TO 6 SERVINGS*	**ACTIVE TIME:** *20 MINUTES*	**START TO FINISH:** *5½ TO 6½ HOURS*

*This dish is heavenly on a crisp fall day with warm
bread and a glass of dry hard cider or warm apple cider.*

3½ POUNDS BONELESS OR BONE-IN
    PORK SHOULDER

1 POUND BABY RAINBOW CARROTS,
    HALVED LENGTHWISE; OR
    REGULAR CARROTS, PEELED AND
    CUT INTO 4-INCH PIECES

5 CELERY STALKS, WASHED AND CUT
    INTO 4-INCH PIECES

2 TO 3 LARGE YELLOW ONIONS, PEELED
    AND QUARTERED

2 GRANNY SMITH APPLES, CORED AND
    CUT INTO 24 WEDGES

1 CINNAMON STICK

4 TO 5 GARLIC CLOVES, CRUSHED

1 TABLESPOON KOSHER SALT

1 TABLESPOON CRACKED BLACK
    PEPPER

2 TABLESPOONS APPLE CIDER VINEGAR

1½ CUPS VEGETABLE OR CHICKEN
    STOCK

2 STAR ANISE PODS

3 BAY LEAVES

1 TABLESPOON CORIANDER SEED

1 TEASPOON SALT

1 TO 2 TABLESPOONS BLACK PEPPER,
    COARSELY GROUND

Add all of the ingredients to the crock-pot. You want to rest the pork shoulder on the top of all the vegetables.

Cover and cook for 5 to 6 hours on low, or until the pork is tender.

Remove the cinnamon stick, star anise, and bay leaves. Ladle the vegetables and some of the juice into a bowl. Remove the pork shoulder and shred into large pieces with a fork. Serve with the pieces of pork shoulder on top of the vegetables.

Tip: Using bone-in pork shoulder will add extra flavor. Just be sure to remove the bone while the dish is still warm so it comes out easily.

POZOLE ROJO

YIELD: *6 SERVINGS*	ACTIVE TIME: *30 MINUTES*	START TO FINISH: *6½ TO 8½ HOURS*

Making this has become my tradition on Cinco de Mayo, as I can set it up in the morning, enjoy the festivities, and then unwind with a delicious meal.

2 CUPS WATER

3 PASILLA PEPPERS, SEEDED

8 ÁRBOL CHILIES, SEEDED

2 TABLESPOONS VEGETABLE OIL

2 POUNDS PORK SHOULDER, CUT INTO 1-INCH CUBES

1 LARGE YELLOW ONION, DICED

3 TABLESPOONS CUMIN

6 GARLIC CLOVES, MINCED

3 TABLESPOONS DRIED OREGANO

5 DASHES TABASCO

3 TABLESPOONS KOSHER SALT

5 CUPS CHICKEN STOCK

1 GREEN BELL PEPPER, SEEDED AND DICED

In a cast-iron skillet, bring the water to a boil. Place the Pasilla peppers and árbol chilies in a bowl, pour the boiling water over them, and cover with plastic wrap. Set aside for 30 minutes, until the chilies are soft.

Place the vegetable oil in the skillet and warm it over medium-high heat. Add the pork, being careful not to overcrowd the pan, and sear for 3 minutes per side. Transfer the seared pork to the crock-pot.

Add the onion, cumin, garlic, oregano, Tabasco, salt, and chicken stock to the crock-pot.

Place the green pepper, Pasilla peppers, árbol chilies, and the water in a blender and puree until smooth. Add the sauce to the crock-pot and cook on high for 6 to 8 hours, until the pork is extremely tender.

Tip: Step 2 is optional but highly recommended. Searing the meat first will help cook off some of the fat before adding it to the pot, which will keep the soup from being too greasy. If you are going to skip this step, try to remove as much of the fat as possible from the pork before adding it to the crock-pot and add 2 hours to the cooking time.

TURKEY CORN CHOWDER

YIELD: *6 SERVINGS*	**ACTIVE TIME:** *25 MINUTES*	**START TO FINISH:** *6 HOURS AND 25 MINUTES*

While chicken is typically the poultry of choice for this recipe, I feel that turkey lends a better texture to this dish. Don't be shy with the bacon, as its salty smokiness is what ties this chowder together.

1 WHITE ONION, PEELED AND
DICED

4 TABLESPOONS FLOUR

1½ POUNDS FINGERLING
POTATOES, SLICED INTO
¼-INCH COINS

4 CUPS CHICKEN STOCK

3 EARS OF CORN

2 POUNDS TURKEY TENDERLOIN,
DICED

¼ CUP CORNSTARCH

2 TABLESPOONS WATER

½ STICK SALTED BUTTER

1½ CUPS LIGHT CREAM

SALT AND PEPPER TO TASTE

BACON, COOKED AND CRUMBLED,
FOR GARNISH

PARSLEY, CHOPPED, FOR GARNISH

Place the onion, flour, and potatoes in the crock-pot. Stir to coat and then add the stock. Continue to stir to prevent lumps from forming.

Remove the corn kernels from the cobs and add to the pot. Cut the corn cobs in half and add to the crock-pot.

Add the turkey and cook on low for 5 hours.

After 5 hours, remove the corn cobs from the crock-pot and discard.

Combine the cornstarch with 2 tablespoons of water and stir until combined.

Add the cornstarch mixture, butter, and cream to the crockpot. Stir, cover, and cook for 1 hour.

Ladle into bowls, garnish with bacon and parsley, if desired, and serve.

SHREDDED CHICKEN WITH BLACK BEANS AND RICE

YIELD: *6 SERVINGS*	ACTIVE TIME: *10 MINUTES*	START TO FINISH: *5 TO 6 HOURS*

The cumin and the jalapeño combine to add depth
to a simple bowl of chicken and rice.

2 POUNDS BONELESS, SKINLESS
    CHICKEN BREASTS

1 CUP CHICKEN STOCK

2 JALAPEÑO PEPPERS (1 SEEDED
    AND MINCED; 1 SEEDED,
    SLICED, AND RESERVED FOR
    GARNISH)

2 GARLIC CLOVES, MINCED

1½ TABLESPOONS CUMIN

1 TABLESPOON GRANULATED
    GARLIC

1 CUP WHITE RICE

2 PLUM TOMATOES, DICED, PLUS
    MORE FOR GARNISH

2 TABLESPOONS KOSHER SALT

1 TABLESPOON BLACK PEPPER

½ POUND BLACK BEANS, COOKED

Place the chicken, chicken stock, jalapeño, garlic, cumin, and granulated garlic in a crock-pot. Cook on high for about 4 hours, until the chicken is tender and falling apart. Remove the chicken, place it in a bowl, and shred it with a fork.

Add the rice, tomatoes, salt, and pepper to the slow cooker and cook until the rice is tender, about 1 hour. Make sure to check the rice for doneness after 45 minutes, as crock-pot cook times vary.

Add the black beans and stir. Top with the shredded chicken and cover to warm. Garnish with diced tomatoes and the jalapeño slices and serve.

CHICKEN AND SAUSAGE CACCIATORE WITH RICE

YIELD: *6 SERVINGS*	**ACTIVE TIME:** *25 MINUTES*	**START TO FINISH:** *6 HOURS AND 15 MINUTES*

Tender chicken thighs, sweet Italian sausage soft enough to cut with a fork, oregano, and a scoop of salty Parmesan cheese combine to create a mouthwatering main course.

1 POUND SWEET ITALIAN SAUSAGE LINKS

6 BONELESS, SKINLESS CHICKEN THIGHS

1 (28 OZ.) CAN WHOLE SAN MARZANO TOMATOES

1 (28 OZ.) CAN DICED TOMATOES; OR 4 BEEFSTEAK TOMATOES, DICED

⅔ CUP DRY RED WINE (CABERNET SAUVIGNON OR MERLOT RECOMMENDED)

4 SHALLOTS, PEELED AND DICED

3 GARLIC CLOVES, PEELED AND MINCED

1 GREEN BELL PEPPER, SEEDED AND DICED

1 RED, YELLOW, OR ORANGE BELL PEPPER, SEEDED AND DICED

¼ CUP DRIED OREGANO, 3 TEASPOONS RESERVED

1 TABLESPOON GRANULATED GARLIC

1 TABLESPOON SUGAR

2 TABLESPOONS KOSHER SALT

½ TEASPOON CRUSHED RED PEPPER FLAKES

1 CUP WHITE RICE

SALT AND PEPPER TO TASTE

PARMESAN CHEESE, GRATED, FOR TOPPING

Place all of the ingredients, besides the white rice, reserved oregano, salt, pepper, and the Parmesan, in the crock-pot and cook on low for 5 hours and 20 minutes.

Add the rice to the crock-pot, raise heat to high, and cook for another 40 to 50 minutes, or until rice is tender. The cooking time may vary depending on your crock-pot, so be sure to check after about 30 minutes to avoid overcooking the rice.

Add the remaining oregano and season with salt and pepper. Top with lots of Parmesan cheese and serve.

Tip: To add another layer of flavor, sear the chicken and sausage before adding them to the crock-pot.

PORTUGUESE CHOURICO
AND KALE SOUP

| YIELD: *6 SERVINGS* | ACTIVE TIME: *25 MINUTES* | START TO FINISH: *5 HOURS* |

There are a ton of variations for this soup, but this version is my absolute favorite. Portuguese chourico is less spicy than Mexican chorizo and uses different seasonings. If you cannot manage to track it down, andouille sausage is a good substitute.

1 POUND PORTUGUESE CHOURICO

3 YELLOW POTATOES, WASHED
AND DICED

½ WHITE ONION, PEELED AND
DICED

4 CUPS CHICKEN STOCK

1 TABLESPOON GRANULATED
GARLIC

1 TABLESPOON PAPRIKA

3 CUPS KALE LEAVES, WASHED
AND TORN BY HAND

SALT AND PEPPER TO TASTE

Place all of the ingredients, besides the kale, in the crock-pot and cook on high for 3 hours and 30 minutes. Add the kale and cook for an additional hour.

Tip: If you want a little bit more action in this soup, you can add kidney beans, cream, and/or carrots.

SAUSAGE WITH PURPLE POTATOES AND SAUERKRAUT

YIELD: *4 TO 6 SERVINGS*	**ACTIVE TIME:** *15 MINUTES*	**START TO FINISH:** *3½ TO 4½ HOURS*

No need to fly to Germany, you can have your own version of Oktoberfest at home. The tangy homemade sauerkraut and the juicy snap of the sausage guarantee people will be feeling festive.

2 TO 3 POUNDS KIELBASA (YOUR FAVORITE KIND OF SAUSAGE WILL WORK, TOO)

2½ POUNDS RED CABBAGE, SLICED THIN

1 CUP RAW APPLE CIDER VINEGAR

¼ CUP SUGAR

2 TABLESPOONS CARAWAY SEEDS

2 TABLESPOONS KOSHER SALT

4 TO 6 SMALL PURPLE POTATOES

WATER OR BEER TO COVER THE CABBAGE

MUSTARD

Place all of the ingredients in a crock-pot with the kielbasa or sausages sitting on top of the cabbage and potatoes. Cover and cook on high for 3 to 4 hours, until the cabbage has softened and taken on a slightly tangy taste. Serve with mustard.

Tips: Bratwurst and knockwurst are good options if you don't want to use kielbasa.

If you're going to go with beer to cover the cabbage, use a pilsner or a lager.

CHIPOTLE SAUSAGE AND PEPPERS

YIELD: *6 SERVINGS*	**ACTIVE TIME:** *10 TO 15 MINUTES*	**START TO FINISH:** *4 HOURS AND 15 MINUTES*

The smoky bite of the chipotle peppers puts a new twist on a ballpark favorite. Serve in a sub roll with some shredded cheese and your favorite hot sauce.

5 BELL PEPPERS, SEEDED AND
SLICED (COMBINATION OF
RED, ORANGE, AND GREEN)

2 CUPS CANNED, STEWED
TOMATOES

3 GARLIC CLOVES

2 CHIPOTLE PEPPERS IN ADOBO

1 TABLESPOON ADOBO SAUCE

2 POUNDS POLISH SAUSAGE, CUT
INTO 6 EVEN PIECES

1 HABANERO PEPPER, PIERCED
BUT NOT CUT

Place the bell peppers in the crock-pot and cook on high heat.

In a blender, add the tomatoes, garlic, chipotle peppers, and adobo sauce and puree. Pour over the peppers and stir to combine.

Add the sausage and the habanero to the crock-pot. Cover and cook on high for 4 hours.

Tip: Canned chipotles in adobo usually come in small 7 oz. cans and are great to have around. They come in handy anytime you want to add a little smoke and spice without going overboard on the heat.

SLOW MARINARA

| YIELD: *6 QUARTS* | ACTIVE TIME: *20 MINUTES* | START TO FINISH: *6½ TO 8½ HOURS* |

This is one of my favorite sauces due to its versatility. I use it as a base for a lot of recipes. Plus, if you add a little bit of cream, you have an Italian tomato bisque. You can also freeze this sauce in batches for a quick pasta fix after a busy day.

3 (28 OZ.) CANS PEELED SAN MARZANO TOMATOES

1 MEDIUM YELLOW ONION, MINCED

4 TO 6 GARLIC CLOVES, MINCED

2 TABLESPOONS GRANULATED SUGAR

2 TABLESPOONS KOSHER SALT

1 TABLESPOON DRIED OREGANO

1 TEASPOON DRIED BASIL

1 TEASPOON CRACKED BLACK PEPPER

1 TEASPOON GRANULATED ONION

1 TEASPOON GRANULATED GARLIC

½ TEASPOON CRUSHED RED PEPPER FLAKES

½ TEASPOON FRESH NUTMEG, GROUND

1 CUP RED WINE

7 TABLESPOONS EXTRA VIRGIN OLIVE OIL

¼ CUP FRESH BASIL, CHOPPED

Add the tomatoes to the crock-pot and crush by hand. Add the remaining ingredients, except for the basil, and cook for 4 hours on high or 6 hours on low.

Once the sauce is done cooking, add the basil and serve.

Tips: I like using San Marzano tomatoes for their natural sweetness. If you are not using them, add an additional tablespoon of sugar to the recipe.

I prefer getting whole tomatoes and crushing them for a chunkier sauce, but if you prefer a smoother sauce you can use tomato puree or puree the tomatoes yourself. If you are using a regular blender to puree your tomatoes after they've cooked, be careful. When blending hot liquids, remember to leave to top of the blender open slightly so that the pressure inside doesn't build up and send hot sauce over everything! I usually leave the top vent on my blender open and cover the opening with a towel to allow steam to escape.

RATATOUILLE

| **YIELD:** *4 TO 6 SERVINGS* | **ACTIVE TIME:** *20 MINUTES* | **START TO FINISH:** *8 HOURS AND 20 MINUTES* |

This is one of the simplest dishes I know and it is such a great, healthy meal. Enjoy it with a baguette topped with butter and a glass of red wine.

1 EGGPLANT, DICED

1 RED BELL PEPPER, DICED

3 ROMA OR PLUM TOMATOES, DICED

1 SMALL ZUCCHINI, DICED

1 SMALL SUMMER SQUASH, DICED

1 YELLOW ONION, DICED

3 GARLIC CLOVES, MINCED

3 SPRIGS OF THYME, LEAVES REMOVED FROM STEM

3 SPRIGS OF OREGANO

3 TABLESPOONS EXTRA VIRGIN OLIVE OIL

1 TABLESPOON FENNEL SEEDS

SALT AND PEPPER TO TASTE

1 BAGUETTE, SLICED

Place all of the ingredients in a crock-pot. Stir to combine, cover, and cook on low for 8 hours. Serve with slices of baguette.

Tip: You can cook this and let it cool overnight in the pot: the flavors will be even better. Just remember to heat it up the next day before serving.

SIMPLE BLACK BEAN SOUP

YIELD: *4 TO 6 SERVINGS*	**ACTIVE TIME:** *10 MINUTES*	**START TO FINISH:** *4 TO 24 HOURS*

*There is something comforting about the simplicity of black bean soup.
For having only a few ingredients, it packs a lot of flavor. My favorite part of making
this soup for company is having the garnishes for everyone to build their own version.
It definitely adds to the excitement.*

1 POUND DRIED BLACK BEANS

1 MEDIUM WHITE OR YELLOW
ONION, DICED

¼ CUP CILANTRO, CHOPPED

1 TO 2 BAY LEAVES

1 TABLESPOON SALT

2 TABLESPOONS CUMIN

2 TABLESPOONS GRANULATED
GARLIC OR 4 TO 5 GARLIC
CLOVES, MINCED

4 CUPS WATER

1 JALAPEÑO PEPPER, SLICED, FOR
GARNISH

CILANTRO, CHOPPED, FOR
GARNISH

1 RADISH, SLICED, FOR GARNISH

HOT SAUCE, FOR GARNISH

CHEDDAR CHEESE, SHREDDED,
FOR GARNISH

LIME WEDGES, FOR GARNISH

Place the black beans in a container and cover with 1 inch of water. Let soak overnight. Once soaked, drain off the liquid and rinse the beans before putting them in the crock-pot.

Add the remaining ingredients to the crock-pot and cook on low for 4 hours.

After 4 hours, check the beans. If you are able to mash them with your fingers, they are done.

Garnish and enjoy.

Tip: Depending on your preference, you can leave the soup chunky or you can use an immersion blender to puree it to a velvety texture.

LOADED BAKED POTATO SOUP

| **YIELD:** *6 SERVINGS* | **ACTIVE TIME:** *15 MINUTES* | **START TO FINISH:** *5 TO 8 HOURS* |

This is the perfect dish for tailgating and it takes almost no time to put together. Thanks to an endless amount of potential topping combinations, it's sure to be everyone's favorite.

4 LARGE BAKING POTATOES, SCRUBBED AND CUT INTO 2-INCH CHUNKS (PEELING OPTIONAL)

4 CUPS LOW-SODIUM CHICKEN STOCK

5 TABLESPOONS BUTTER

½ YELLOW ONION, DICED

1 TABLESPOON GRANULATED GARLIC

1 TABLESPOON KOSHER SALT

1 TABLESPOON BLACK PEPPER

¼ CUP SCALLIONS, WHITES MINCED, GREENS RESERVED FOR TOPPING

1 CUP HALF-AND-HALF

1 CUP CHEDDAR CHEESE, SHREDDED

Add all of the ingredients, besides the half-and-half and cheddar cheese to the crock-pot, and cook for 4 to 5 hours on high until the potatoes are soft enough to mash.

Once the potatoes are soft, add the half-and-half and cheese and stir.

If looking for a smoother texture, puree with an immersion blender. If you are looking for a chunkier texture, use a hand masher. Ladle into bowls, top with the scallion greens and other preferred toppings, and serve.

If crispy bacon is one of the things you want on top, heat the oven to 375°F. Place a cooling rack on a rimmed baking pan and place a single layer of bacon on the rack. Depending on the thickness of your bacon, cook for 20 to 30 minutes, while spinning halfway through. To make crispy fried shallots, thinly slice shallots and toss in flour seasoned with salt and pepper. Shake off the excess flour and fry in 375°F oil for about 1 minute, or until the shallots turn slightly brown. Remove from oil and place on a paper towel-lined tray or plate. While the shallots are still hot, sprinkle with seasoning(s) of your choice.

Tips: A number of toppings work for this soup. Some of my favorites are bacon, scallion greens, chives, Greek yogurt, sour cream, shredded cheese, broccoli, and crispy fried shallots.

If you do not have an immersion blender, you can puree the soup in batches with a normal blender. Just be careful not to fill the blender too much. Leave the small top cover off and use a towel to cover, leaving enough room for steam to escape. This will ensure that the lid of the blender does not pop off and leave you with a considerable mess.

MOROCCAN LENTIL STEW

YIELD: *6 SERVINGS*	**ACTIVE TIME:** *15 TO 25 MINUTES*	**START TO FINISH:** *6 HOURS AND 30 MINUTES*

This vegetarian dish is incredibly filling thanks to the lentils.

1 CUP BROWN LENTILS

½ CUP FRENCH LENTILS

4 CUPS CHICKEN OR VEGETABLE
STOCK

3 CARROTS, WASHED AND DICED

1 LARGE WHITE ONION, PEELED
AND DICED

3 GARLIC CLOVES, PEELED AND
MINCED

3 TABLESPOONS FRESH GINGER,
PEELED AND MINCED

ZEST AND JUICE OF 1 LEMON

3 TABLESPOONS SMOKED PAPRIKA

1½ TABLESPOONS FRESH
CINNAMON, GRATED; OR
2 TABLESPOONS GROUND
CINNAMON

1 TABLESPOON GROUND
CORIANDER

1 TABLESPOON TURMERIC

1 TABLESPOON CUMIN

½ TABLESPOON ALLSPICE

2 TO 3 BAY LEAVES

SALT AND PEPPER TO TASTE

2 CUPS WHITE BEANS, COOKED

FRESH MINT, FOR GARNISH

GOAT CHEESE, CRUMBLED, FOR
GARNISH

Place the lentils in a fine sieve and rinse to remove any impurities.

Place all of the ingredients, besides the white beans and the garnishes, in a crock-pot. Cover and cook on low for 7½ hours.

After 7½ hours, add the cooked white beans. Stir, cover, and cook for 30 minutes.

Garnish with fresh mint and goat cheese and serve.

Tip: Using fresh and whole spices makes all the difference when it comes to flavor. If your dry spices have been in your cabinet for more than a year, chances are they have lost their potency and need to be replaced. Stocking up on whole spices will help preserve freshness and flavor. Invest in a small spice grinder or an electric coffee grinder and you'll always have fresh spices on hand.

SPINACH AND MUSHROOM QUINOA WITH FRESH HERBS

YIELD: *6 SERVINGS*	ACTIVE TIME: *15 TO 20 MINUTES*	START TO FINISH: *4½ TO 5½ HOURS*

Folding in the herbs at the end of your preparation
gives this dish tons of fresh flavor.

1½ CUPS QUINOA, WASHED

2½ CUPS CHICKEN STOCK (OR
   YOUR PREFERRED STOCK)

1 YELLOW ONION, PEELED AND
   DICED

½ RED BELL PEPPER, DICED

¾ POUND BABY PORTOBELLO
   MUSHROOMS, CLEANED AND
   ROUGHLY CHOPPED

2 GARLIC CLOVES, PEELED AND
   MINCED

1 TABLESPOON KOSHER SALT

1 TABLESPOON BLACK PEPPER,
   FRESHLY CRACKED, PLUS
   MORE TO TASTE

3 CUPS BABY SPINACH

1½ CUPS FRESH BASIL, CHOPPED

¼ CUP FRESH DILL, CHOPPED

⅛ CUP FRESH THYME LEAVES

SALT TO TASTE

Place all of the ingredients, besides the spinach and fresh herbs, in your crock-pot. Cook on high for 4 hours. After 4 hours, check the quinoa for doneness. It should be slightly fluffy.

When the quinoa is fluffy, add the spinach and turn off the heat. Keep the crock-pot covered and let sit for 1 hour.

Fluff with a fork and fold in the basil, dill, and thyme. Season with salt and pepper and serve.

Tip: For added flavor, sauté your vegetables for 5 to 10 minutes over high heat, stirring often to prevent them from burning. Cook until slightly caramelized before adding to the crock-pot. To maintain the proper level of moisture, add another ¼ cup of stock to the crock-pot.

CAST-IRON

Like many people who spend a lot of time in the kitchen, a cast-iron skillet is one of my favorite pieces of cookware. Able to move effortlessly between the stovetop and oven and capable of withstanding the considerable heat of a grill or campfire, its versatility is unmatched. It also distributes and holds heat very well, meaning you can trust it to provide consistent results time after time. When it comes time to clean your cast-iron, make sure you stay away from soap. Instead, add a little water and scrub it with the tough side of a sponge. Wipe it out with paper towel, rub it with a little vegetable oil and salt, and pop it in an oven to dry at 200°F.

STRIP STEAK WITH MUSHROOMS AND FINGERLING POTATOES

YIELD: *6 SERVINGS*	**ACTIVE TIME:** *30 MINUTES*	**START TO FINISH:** *1 HOUR AND 30 MINUTES*

I have to admit, I'm not always the biggest steak fan. But I can get on board when it's cooked in a cast-iron skillet and smothered in butter. Once you get this recipe down, there's no reason to ever visit that fancy local steak house again.

- 2 TABLESPOONS KOSHER SALT OR COARSE SEA SALT
- ½ TEASPOON CRUSHED RED PEPPER FLAKES
- ½ TEASPOON GROUND BLACK PEPPER
- ½ TEASPOON FENNEL SEEDS
- ½ TEASPOON MUSTARD SEEDS
- ½ TEASPOON CORIANDER SEEDS
- 6 (7 OZ.) STRIP LOIN STEAKS
- 2 POUNDS FINGERLING POTATOES, HALVED LENGTHWISE
- 2 TABLESPOONS OLIVE OIL
- ¾ CUP UNSALTED BUTTER AT ROOM TEMPERATURE, CUT INTO 7 CHUNKS
- 6 SPRIGS OF THYME, PLUS 2 TABLESPOONS OF LEAVES FOR GARNISH
- 1 LARGE SHALLOT, MINCED
- 2 POUNDS CREMINI MUSHROOMS, CLEANED AND QUARTERED OR CUT IN 6 PIECES
- 1 POUND SHIITAKE MUSHROOMS, STEMS REMOVED AND THIN SLICED
- 1 POUND OYSTER MUSHROOMS, SLICED THIN
- ½ CUP CABERNET SAUVIGNON
- 2 TABLESPOONS LITE TAMARI OR LITE SOY SAUCE
- ¼ CUP WORCESTERSHIRE SAUCE
- 2 TABLESPOONS FISH SAUCE

Preheat oven to 375°F.

Place the salt, red pepper flakes, and ground black pepper in a bowl. Use a coffee grinder or a mortar and pestle to grind the fennel seeds, mustard seeds, and coriander seeds into a powder. Place the powder in the bowl with the salt, red pepper flakes, and ground black pepper and stir to combine.

Place steaks on a plate and season liberally with the seasoning blend. Set the steaks aside and let stand for 1 hour.

Place the potatoes in a cast-iron skillet and cover with water. Cook over high heat until the potatoes are tender but not mushy. Drain and set aside.

Continued...

Tips:

For a 1-inch thick steak, 2 minutes on each side should get you to a perfect rare to medium rare.

Take whatever butter you have left over and mix it with some chopped thyme leaves. Place this on the steaks and enjoy.

Wipe the skillet, add the olive oil, and warm over medium-high heat. Add the steaks to the pan, making sure you don't overcrowd. Cook steaks for 2 minutes, turn them over, and add 1 chunk of butter and 1 sprig of thyme for each steak. Cook steaks for 2 minutes, while spooning the butter over the steaks. Remove steaks and set aside. Remove thyme sprigs and discard.

Add the shallot and the remaining chunk of butter to the pan. Cook for 1 minute and add the cremini mushrooms. Cook for 5 minutes and then add the shiitake and oyster mushrooms. Cook for 3 more minutes and add the Cabernet Sauvignon. After 30 seconds, add the potatoes, Worcestershire sauce, tamari or soy sauce, and fish sauce. Stir until the mushrooms are evenly coated.

Return the steaks and their juices to the skillet. Place the skillet in the oven and cook for 3 minutes, until the steaks are warmed through.

Remove the skillet from the oven and slice the steaks at a 45° angle every 2 inches. Scoop the potatoes and vegetables onto a plate, top with the sliced steak, sprinkle with the fresh thyme leaves, and serve.

CHIMICHURRI STRIP STEAK WITH OREGANO POTATOES AND ONIONS

YIELD: *4 SERVINGS*	**ACTIVE TIME:** *20 MINUTES*	**START TO FINISH:** *24 HOURS*

I have worked in a few different restaurants where some of the kitchen staff was from South America. No matter what country they came from, they always seemed to whip up some version of this Argentinian dish for the staff meal. Serve it with a simple salad of tomatoes, cucumbers, greens, and onions, you'll see why I fell in love with it.

STEAK, POTATOES, AND ONIONS

4 (5 TO 6 OZ.) N.Y. STRIP STEAKS

1 POUND WHITE SWEET POTATOES, PEELED AND DICED

1 POUND YUKON GOLD POTATOES, PEELED AND DICED

1 TABLESPOON OF SALT, PLUS MORE TO TASTE

1 TABLESPOON OLIVE OIL

2 TABLESPOONS BEEF TALLOW

1 LARGE WHITE ONION, SLICED THIN

BLACK PEPPER TO TASTE

¼ CUP WHITE VINEGAR OR RED WINE VINEGAR

⅓ CUP DRY RED WINE (CABERNET SAUVIGNON, TEMPRANILLO, OR RIOJA)

1 TABLESPOON FRESH OREGANO, CHOPPED

Continued...

STEAK, POTATOES, AND ONIONS

Transfer half of the Chimichurri Sauce (see page 105) and the steaks to a container and let them marinate in the refrigerator overnight. Refrigerate the other half of the sauce in a separate container.

Preheat oven to 375°F.

Remove the steaks from the marinade and season both sides with salt. Set aside and let come to room temperature as you cook the potatoes and onions.

Place the white sweet potatoes, the Yukon Gold potatoes, and salt in a large cast-iron pan. Cover with water, bring to a boil, and cook until the potatoes are tender. Drain and set aside.

Wipe the pan, add the olive oil and beef tallow, and warm over medium-high heat. Add the steaks and cook for 2 minutes on each side. Remove the steaks from the pan and set aside.

Place the potatoes, onion, 3 tablespoons of chimichurri sauce, salt, and pepper in the pan and cook over medium heat while stirring. Cook for approximately 10 minutes until the onion is cooked through. Add the vinegar, wine, and oregano and cook for 5 minutes, or until the vinegar and wine have nearly evaporated.

Return the steaks to the pan and place it in the oven for 5 minutes.

Remove the pan from the oven, divide between serving plates, top with the remaining chimichurri sauce, and serve with a small salad.

CHIMICHURRI SAUCE

2 TABLESPOONS FRESH OREGANO

4 TABLESPOONS EXTRA VIRGIN
    OLIVE OIL

2 CUPS FRESH PARSLEY

1½ CUPS FRESH CILANTRO

1 SMALL WHITE OR YELLOW
    ONION, CHOPPED

2 SCALLIONS

1 JALAPEÑO PEPPER (SEEDS
    REMOVED IF YOU DON'T
    WANT THE EXTRA HEAT)

¼ TABLESPOON SALT

¼ TABLESPOON PEPPER

¼ TABLESPOON ONION POWDER

¼ TABLESPOON GARLIC POWDER

1 TABLESPOON SUGAR

⅓ CUP WATER

CHIMICHURRI SAUCE

Place all of the ingredients in a blender and puree until smooth.

Tips: White sweet potatoes are mild in flavor. They also have a softer skin than the orange variety, which allows them to cook evenly with the other potatoes in this dish.

Beef tallow is the rendered fat of beef, and is a great substitute for butter. If you are feeling adventurous and want the authentic taste of this dish, you can ask your local butcher for some beef fat, grind it in a food processor until fine, and cook it in a crock-pot for 6 to 8 hours. Then strain the fat through a coffee filter and store the liquid in the refrigerator until ready to use. To get 1 cup of tallow, you'll need 1 pound of beef fat.

STEAK AND PEARL ONION FRITTATA

YIELD: *6 SERVINGS*	**ACTIVE TIME:** *10 MINUTES*	**START TO FINISH:** *25 MINUTES*

Frittatas are traditionally enjoyed at breakfast, but this one is hearty enough to work any time of day. A slice of this with an arugula and red onion salad is one of my favorite dinners when I'm pressed for time.

2 TABLESPOONS OLIVE OIL

1 POUND PEARL ONIONS

SALT AND PEPPER TO TASTE

12 LARGE EGGS

½ CUP HEAVY CREAM OR HALF-AND-HALF

1 (7 TO 8 OZ.) STRIP STEAK, MINCED

4 TABLESPOONS UNSALTED BUTTER

2 TABLESPOONS FRESH PARSLEY, CHOPPED

2 CUPS PARMESAN OR ASIAGO CHEESE, SHREDDED

Preheat oven to 400°F. Place your cast-iron skillet over medium-high heat and add the olive oil. Once the pan is hot, add the pearl onions, salt, and pepper and cook until onions are starting to caramelize, about 5 to 7 minutes.

While the onions are cooking, place the eggs, cream, salt, and pepper in a bowl and scramble until combined.

Add the steak to the pan with the onions and cook until steak is cooked through, about 2 to 3 minutes. Add the butter and parsley and stir until the butter is melted. Sprinkle the cheese evenly over the onions and steak then pour the egg mixture into the pan. The eggs should just cover everything else in the pan. Place the skillet in the oven and cook for 8 minutes.

Turn the broiler on and cook for another 3 minutes, until the top of the frittata is brown. Remove from the oven and serve.

Tip: Pearl onions can be found in the frozen section of most supermarkets if fresh are unavailable. But if you can find fresh, the same trick that works for peeling cipollini onions (see page 129) also comes in handy when dealing with fresh pearl onions.

CHICKEN PICCATA

YIELD: *6 SERVINGS*	ACTIVE TIME: *30 MINUTES*	START TO FINISH: *45 MINUTES*

The mushrooms give this traditional piccata a little boost, as their mellow flavor complements the lemon's tartness and the saltiness of the capers.

12 OZ. ANGEL HAIR PASTA

1 STICK OF BUTTER, QUARTERED

¾ CUP EXTRA VIRGIN OLIVE OIL

1 CUP FLOUR, PLUS 2
    TABLESPOONS

SALT AND PEPPER TO TASTE

1½ POUNDS BONELESS, SKINLESS
    CHICKEN BREASTS, CUT INTO
    ¼-POUND CUTLETS

1¼ CUPS CREMINI MUSHROOMS,
    CLEANED AND SLICED

3 GARLIC CLOVES, MINCED

½ CUP SHALLOTS, MINCED

2 CUPS CHICKEN STOCK

⅓ CUP LEMON JUICE

⅓ CUP CAPERS AND THEIR BRINE

2 CUPS PARSLEY, WASHED AND
    CHOPPED

Fill a large cast-iron skillet with water, add a pinch of salt, and bring to a boil. Add the pasta and cook until al dente. Drain and set aside.

Place the pan over medium-high heat. Add ¼ of the butter and ⅓ of the oil. While the skillet is warming, combine 1 cup of the flour, salt, and pepper in a bowl and then dredge the chicken breasts in it.

Place half of the chicken in the skillet and cook until each side is golden brown and the center temperature is 155°F. Remove chicken breasts and set aside. Repeat with the remaining pieces of chicken.

Add some water to the skillet and use a wooden spoon to scrape any burned bits off the bottom of the skillet. Drain and place the skillet back on the stove.

Add another ¼ of the butter and the remaining oil to the skillet. Once the butter melts, add the mushrooms and cook for 5 minutes while stirring often. Add the garlic and shallots and cook for another 2 minutes, until the shallots are translucent and the garlic is fragrant.

Add the remaining flour to the skillet, stir, and scrape the skillet to coat the mushroom mixture. Cook for about 2 minutes and then add the chicken stock. Stir and scrape the skillet until the sauce starts to thicken, about 5 minutes. Add the lemon juice, capers and their brine, and the remaining butter. As soon as the butter starts to melt, add the parsley and return the pasta to the skillet. Use tongs to toss the pasta until coated. Return the chicken to the pan and cook until heated through.

CAPRESE CHICKEN BAKE

YIELD: *6 SERVINGS*	ACTIVE TIME: *15 MINUTES*	START TO FINISH: *45 MINUTES*

By tossing a traditional caprese salad between layers of thinly sliced chicken breast, you transform what should be ho-hum ingredients into a dazzling dinner.

1 GARLIC CLOVE, MINCED

1 TEASPOON DRIED OREGANO

1 TEASPOON GRANULATED GARLIC

SALT AND PEPPER TO TASTE

2 TABLESPOONS EXTRA VIRGIN
OLIVE OIL

2 POUNDS BONELESS, SKINLESS
CHICKEN BREASTS, HALVED
ALONG THEIR EQUATOR

2 POUNDS ROMA OR PLUM
TOMATOES, SLICED IN
¼-INCH THICK COINS (YOU
CAN ALSO SUBSTITUTE ANY
TOMATO YOU LIKE)

1 POUND FRESH MOZZARELLA,
SLICED INTO ¼-INCH THICK
PIECES

LEAVES FROM 1 BUNCH OF FRESH
BASIL

BALSAMIC GLAZE OR REDUCTION

Preheat oven to 375°F. Combine the garlic, oregano, granulated garlic, salt, and pepper in a bowl. Place 1 tablespoon of olive oil and the sliced chicken breasts in a bowl and toss to coat. Dredge the chicken breasts in the garlic-and-spice mixture and set aside.

Place the remaining olive oil in a cast-iron skillet and warm it over medium-high heat. Working in batches, sear the chicken breasts for 1 minute per side.

When all of the chicken has been seared, place half of the breasts in an even layer on the bottom of the skillet. Top with ⅔ of the tomatoes and mozzarella and half of the basil leaves. Place the remaining chicken breasts on top and cover with the remaining tomatoes, mozzarella, and basil.

Place the skillet in the oven and cook until the cheese is melted and bubbling, about 10 minutes. The temperature at the center of the chicken breasts should be 165°F. Remove the skillet from the oven and let rest for 10 minutes. Top with balsamic glaze, cut into 6 sections, and serve.

Tip: Balsamic glaze is a great product found at most grocery stores. It can also be made at home by bringing balsamic vinegar to a boil in a small saucepan, reducing the heat, and letting it simmer for 10 to 15 minutes. It is ready when it is thick enough to coat the back of a spoon and has the consistency of melted chocolate. Remove from heat, let it cool, transfer to a jar or a squeeze bottle, and store in your refrigerator.

KOREAN CHICKEN THIGHS WITH SWEET POTATO VERMICELLI

YIELD: *4 TO 6 SERVINGS*	**ACTIVE TIME:** *45 MINUTES*	**START TO FINISH:** *3 HOURS AND 30 MINUTES*

This is a Korean take on lo mein, the Chinese Classic. The umami flavor of the sweet potato noodles, shiitake mushrooms, and cabbage is the perfect complement to the sweetness of the marinated chicken.

CHICKEN THIGHS AND VERMICELLI

4 TO 6 SKIN-ON, BONE-IN CHICKEN THIGHS (IF YOU PLAN ON CHOPPING THE CHICKEN, YOU CAN GO WITH BONELESS)

2 TABLESPOONS VEGETABLE OIL

¼ HEAD OF NAPA CABBAGE, CHOPPED

3½ OZ. SHIITAKE MUSHROOMS, SLICED THIN

1 SHALLOT, PEELED AND SLICED THIN

1 YELLOW ONION, PEELED AND SLICED THIN

2 GARLIC CLOVES, MINCED

2 SCALLIONS, WHITES CHOPPED, GREENS RESERVED

2 TABLESPOONS GINGER, PEELED AND MINCED

¼ CUP BROWN SUGAR

2 TABLESPOONS SESAME OIL

2 TABLESPOONS FISH SAUCE

¼ CUP SOY SAUCE

¼ CUP RICE VINEGAR

¼ CUP SESAME SEEDS

Continued...

CHICKEN THIGHS AND VERMICELLI

Fill a large cast-iron pan with water and bring to a boil. Add the vermicelli and cook for about 6 minutes. Drain, rinse with cold water to keep them from sticking, and set aside.

Preheat the oven to 375°F. Remove the chicken from the refrigerator and place the cast-iron pan back on the stove. Add the vegetable oil and warm over medium-high heat. Remove the chicken thighs from the marinade and place them skin side down in the pan. Reserve the marinade.

Sear the chicken until a crust forms on the skin, about 5 to 7 minutes. Turn the chicken thighs over, add the reserved marinade, place the pan in the oven, and cook for about 15 to 20 minutes, until the centers of the chicken thighs reach 165°F.

Remove the pan from the oven and set the chicken aside. Drain the pan and wipe it clean. Return to the stove, add the cabbage, mushrooms, shallot, onion, garlic, scallion whites, and ginger and cook for 8 minutes, or until the cabbage is wilted.

Add the brown sugar, sesame oil, fish sauce, soy sauce, and rice vinegar to a small bowl and stir until combined. Add this sauce and the vermicelli to the pan, stir until the noodles are coated, and then return the chicken thighs to the pan. Top with the scallion greens and sesame seeds, return to the oven for 5 minutes, and serve.

Continued...

MARINADE

1 STALK OF LEMONGRASS, TENDER
    PART ONLY (THE BOTTOM
    HALF)

2 GARLIC CLOVES, PEELED

1 TABLESPOON FRESH GINGER,
    PEELED

1 SCALLION

¼ CUP BROWN SUGAR

2 TABLESPOONS CHILI PASTE

1 TABLESPOON SESAME OIL

1 TABLESPOON RICE VINEGAR

10 OZ. SWEET POTATO VERMICELLI

2 TABLESPOONS FISH SAUCE

1 TABLESPOON BLACK PEPPER

MARINADE

Place all of the ingredients in a blender and blend until smooth. Pour over the chicken thighs and marinate in the refrigerator for at least 2 hours.

Tip: Sweet potato noodles can be found at most specialty stores and a few major chains. If you can't find them in a store near you, you can order them online.

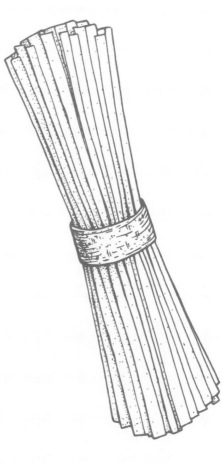

COCONUT CURRY CHICKEN WITH BASMATI RICE

YIELD: *4 TO 6 SERVINGS*	**ACTIVE TIME:** *20 MINUTES*	**START TO FINISH:** *1 HOUR*

The coconut milk tempers the spice in this just enough
to ensure that your experience is pure pleasure.

5 TABLESPOONS GREEN CURRY
PASTE

4 TO 6 BONELESS CHICKEN
THIGHS

2 YELLOW ONIONS, PEELED AND
SLICED ¼-INCH THICK

2 RED BELL PEPPERS, SEEDED AND
SLICED ¼-INCH THICK

3 TABLESPOONS GINGER, PEELED
AND MASHED

1 GARLIC CLOVE, PEELED AND
MASHED

3 TABLESPOONS FISH SAUCE

1 TABLESPOON MADRAS CURRY
POWDER

1 (13½ OZ.) CAN LITE COCONUT
MILK

2 TABLESPOONS THAI BASIL,
CHOPPED, PLUS MORE FOR
GARNISH

1½ CUPS RICE

1 CUP WATER

LIME WEDGES, FOR GARNISH

CILANTRO, CHOPPED, FOR
GARNISH

Preheat oven to 375°F.

Rub 2 tablespoons of the green curry paste on the chicken and set aside for at least 30 minutes. Place a cast-iron skillet over medium-high heat and add the chicken thighs, skin side down. Cook until the skin is crispy, turn over, and cook for another 3 minutes. Remove the chicken from the skillet and set aside.

Add the onions, peppers, ginger, and garlic and cook while stirring for 5 to 7 minutes. As the vegetables and aromatics are cooking, make sure you scrape the bottom of the pan to remove all of the browned bits from the bottom.

Add the remaining green curry paste and cook for an additional 3 minutes, until fragrant.

Add the fish sauce, Madras curry powder, coconut milk, and Thai basil and stir until combined. Add the rice and water, stir, and then return the chicken to the pan. Cover and transfer the pan to the oven. Cook for 25 minutes until the rice is tender and has absorbed all of the liquid. Garnish with the additional Thai basil, lime wedges, and cilantro.

Tip: To mash ginger and garlic, mince them first and then use a mortar and pestle. Make sure you reserve whatever juices are released and add them to the dish.

PORK FRIED RICE

YIELD: *8 SERVINGS*	ACTIVE TIME: *25 MINUTES*	START TO FINISH: *35 MINUTES*

*A comfort food classic using leftovers actually improves this dish.
The next time you order Chinese food, add one or two sides
of white rice and you're halfway to another delicious meal.*

¼ CUP CANOLA OIL (OR
    PREFERRED NEUTRAL OIL)

1 TABLESPOON FRESH GINGER,
    MINCED

1 TABLESPOON FRESH GARLIC,
    MINCED

1 POUND PORK TENDERLOIN,
    COOKED AND DICED

3 TO 4 LARGE EGGS

2 CUPS CARROTS, MINCED

4 CUPS WHITE RICE, COOKED
    (LEFTOVER RICE IS
    PREFERRED)

4 SCALLIONS, CHOPPED

1 CUP FRESH OR FROZEN PEAS

2 TABLESPOONS LITE SOY SAUCE

1 TABLESPOON RICE VINEGAR

1 TABLESPOON FISH SAUCE

1 TABLESPOON SESAME OIL

Place the cooking oil in a cast-iron skillet and cook over medium-high heat until the oil just starts to shimmer. Add the ginger and garlic and cook for about 2 minutes, or until they start to brown.

Raise the heat to high and add the pork. Cook for 5 minutes, or until the pork starts to form a light crust.

Push the meat to one side of the pan and add the eggs. Scramble with a fork until the eggs are cooked through, roughly 2 minutes.

Add the carrots, rice, scallions, and peas and stir to incorporate. Add the soy sauce, rice vinegar, fish sauce, and sesame oil and cook for 5 minutes, stirring constantly.

Tip: Fish sauce has been gaining in popularity over the past several years, and for good reason. If you've been searching for that perfect umami flavor, fish sauce is akin to striking gold. Just be careful not to overdo it. A good rule of thumb: add just enough fish sauce that you can vaguely smell it.

PAELLA

YIELD: *4 TO 6 SERVINGS*	**ACTIVE TIME:** *40 MINUTES*	**START TO FINISH:** *2 HOURS AND 15 MINUTES*

Sure, it's packed with chicken, sausage, and seafood, but the saffron is the true star of this meal. Its subtle, enigmatic flavor is certain to turn heads.

½ CUP PARSLEY, DICED

2 TABLESPOONS EXTRA VIRGIN
OLIVE OIL

1 LEMON, ½ JUICED AND ½ CUT
INTO WEDGES

SALT AND PEPPER TO TASTE

4 TO 6 BONELESS, SKINLESS
CHICKEN THIGHS

16 TO 24 SHRIMP (16/20, TAIL ON)

½ POUND SPANISH CHORIZO

¼ CUP PANCETTA, DICED

½ LARGE WHITE ONION, DICED
(ROUGHLY 1½ CUPS)

1 BELL PEPPER, MINCED

4 GARLIC CLOVES, MINCED

1 CUP ROMA TOMATOES, DICED

3 CUPS SHORT-GRAIN RICE

6 CUPS CHICKEN STOCK

1 TEASPOON SAFFRON

1 TABLESPOON PIMENTON
(SPANISH PAPRIKA)

16 TO 24 PEI MUSSELS, CLEANED

1 CUP PEAS (FRESH IF POSSIBLE)

Preheat the oven to 450°F. Place 2 tablespoons of the parsley, the olive oil, lemon juice, salt, and pepper in a bowl and stir to combine. Add the chicken thighs to the bowl and marinate for 30 minutes to 1 hour.

Heat a cast-iron skillet over medium-high heat. Add the chicken to the pan and sear on each side for 3 to 5 minutes. Remove the chicken from the pan and set aside.

Place the shrimp in the pan and cook for 2 minutes on each side, until the shrimp is cooked approximately ¾ of the way through. Remove shrimp and set aside.

Place the chorizo, pancetta, onion, bell pepper, and half of the garlic in the skillet and cook for 10 to 15 minutes, until the onion is slightly caramelized. Season with salt and pepper and add tomatoes, rice, chicken stock, the remaining garlic and parsley, saffron, and pimenton. Cook for 10 minutes, stirring often.

Reduce heat to medium-low and press the chicken into the contents of the skillet. Cover the skillet with a lid or aluminum foil and cook for 10 minutes.

Uncover the skillet and add the mussels, shrimp, and peas. Cover the skillet, place it in the oven, and cook until the majority of the mussels have opened and the rice is tender. Discard any mussels that have not opened. If the rice is still a bit crunchy, remove the mussels and shrimp, set them aside, return pan to the oven, and cook until the rice is tender. Serve with the lemon wedges.

WALNUT AND BROWN BUTTER SCALLOPS WITH BUTTERNUT SQUASH

YIELD: *4 TO 6 SERVINGS*	ACTIVE TIME: *40 MINUTES*	START TO FINISH: *1 HOUR AND 15 MINUTES*

Here's a delicious and deceptively simple recipe from my friend Mel, who also came up with the New England Clam Chowder recipe (see page 170). The combination of fresh, tender scallops and rich, nutty brown butter is a good way to impress anyone.

24 SCALLOPS (U10)

SALT AND PEPPER TO TASTE

1 STICK UNSALTED BUTTER

2 TABLESPOONS EXTRA VIRGIN OLIVE OIL

3 TO 4 MEDIUM BUTTERNUT SQUASH, PEELED, SEEDED, AND MINCED

1 CUP RAW, SHELLED WALNUTS

SCALLIONS, CHOPPED, FOR GARNISH

Place a cast-iron skillet over medium-high heat. Remove the foot from each scallop and discard. Pat the scallops dry with a paper towel and lightly season both sides with salt and pepper.

Place 1 tablespoon of the butter and the olive oil in the skillet. Add the scallops one at a time, softly pressing down as you place them in the skillet. Cook the scallops for approximately 3 minutes and then flip them over. The scallops should not stick to the skillet when you flip them. If the scallops do stick, cook until a brown crust is visible. Once you have flipped the scallops, cook for 2 minutes, remove, and set aside.

Add the butternut squash, season with salt and pepper, and cook for 12 to 15 minutes, or until they are tender and caramelized. Remove the squash and set aside.

Add the walnuts to the skillet and cook while stirring often for 2 minutes, or until the nuts are fragrant. Add the remaining butter to the skillet and cook for 2 to 3 minutes, until browned.

Place the squash in the middle of a plate and place the scallops around and on top of the squash. Spoon the walnuts and butter over the dish, garnish with the scallions, and serve.

Tips: U10 is a unit of measurement that refers to the amount of scallops per pound, meaning that you will have 10 or fewer.

The foot of a scallop is a ½ x 1-inch milky white piece attached to the side. It can easily be peeled off.

MUSSELS WITH TOMATOES AND ORZO

YIELD: *4 TO 6 SERVINGS*	**ACTIVE TIME:** *30 MINUTES*	**START TO FINISH:** *45 MINUTES*

The subtle sweetness of Prince Edward Island mussels lends this dish tons of flavor, and they are perfectly sized. There's a lot of juice to sop up in this one, so serve with a warm loaf of bread and plenty of napkins.

- 3 POUNDS PEI MUSSELS, WASHED AND SCRUBBED
- 3 TABLESPOONS OLIVE OIL, PLUS MORE FOR GARNISH
- 2 GARLIC CLOVES, PEELED AND SLICED THIN
- 1 LARGE SHALLOT, PEELED AND SLICED THIN
- 4 SCALLIONS, WHITES SLICED THIN, GREENS RESERVED FOR GARNISH
- 1 CUP ORZO, TOASTED
- ¼ CUP SUN-DRIED TOMATOES, THINLY SLICED
- 2 PINTS CHERRY TOMATOES
- 1½ CUPS CHICKEN STOCK
- ½ CUP WHITE WINE
- 2 TABLESPOONS BUTTER
- SALT AND PEPPER TO TASTE
- ½ CUP BASIL, CHOPPED, FOR GARNISH
- LOAF OF CRUSTY BREAD

Remove any open, cracked, or damaged mussels. Use a thin towel to remove the "beards," the brown threads extending from where the two shells meet. Pull the threads toward the hinge until the beard separates from the mussel.

Preheat the oven to 350°F. Heat a cast-iron skillet over medium-high heat and add the oil. When the oil is warm, add the garlic, shallot, and scallion whites and sauté for 3 minutes, stirring constantly. Add the orzo and sun-dried tomatoes and stir to coat. Cook, stirring occasionally for about 10 minutes, until the orzo is slightly toasted.

Add the cherry tomatoes, chicken stock, and white wine and transfer the skillet to the oven. Cook for about 10 minutes, until the orzo is cooked through and the tomatoes begin to split open.

Remove the skillet from the oven and place the hinge of each mussel into the orzo with the openings of the mussels facing upward. Return to the oven and cook for 5 to 7 minutes, until the majority of the mussels are open. Remove from the oven and discard any unopened mussels. Drizzle with olive oil, garnish with the basil and scallion greens, and serve with warm bread.

Tip: When you get the mussels, put them in a bowl of fresh water until you prepare the ingredients for the rest of the dish.

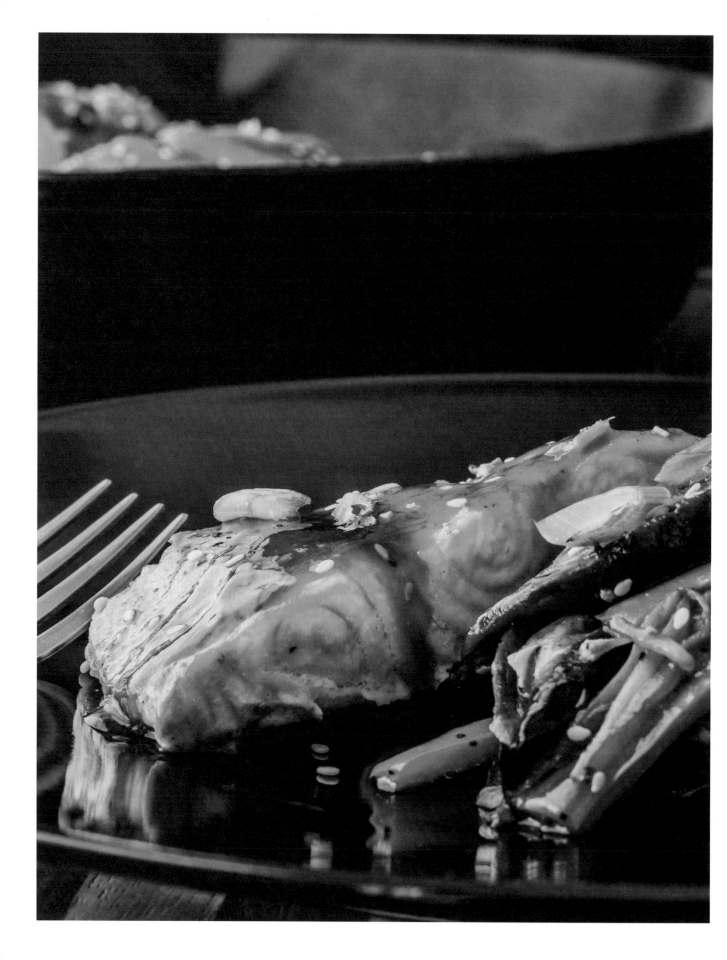

TERIYAKI SALMON WITH CHINESE EGGPLANTS AND BEAN SPROUTS

YIELD: *4 SERVINGS*	ACTIVE TIME: *20 MINUTES*	START TO FINISH: *20 MINUTES*

Seafood was on my no-go list until my early 20s when I met someone who was obsessed with salmon. Since this recipe ended up in the book, it's safe to say they made me see the light.

TERIYAKI SAUCE

1 TABLESPOON FRESH GINGER, PEELED AND MINCED

2 TO 3 GARLIC CLOVES, PEELED AND MINCED

1 TABLESPOON RICE OR WHITE VINEGAR

2 TABLESPOONS LIGHT BROWN SUGAR

¼ CUP LITE SOY SAUCE

1 TABLESPOON TAPIOCA STARCH OR CORNSTARCH

½ CUP WATER

SALMON WITH CHINESE EGGPLANTS AND BEAN SPROUTS

3 TABLESPOONS CANOLA OIL (OR PREFERRED NEUTRAL OIL)

4 CHINESE EGGPLANTS, CUT INTO ½-INCH THICK SLICES ON A BIAS

1 RED BELL PEPPER, SEEDED AND JULIENNED

2 TABLESPOONS SCALLIONS, CHOPPED, GREENS RESERVED FOR GARNISH

1 CUP BEAN SPROUTS

1½ POUNDS ATLANTIC SALMON, SKIN REMOVED

SALT AND PEPPER TO TASTE

TERIYAKI SAUCE

Place all of the ingredients in a blender and puree until smooth. Transfer to a small saucepan and cook while stirring until the sauce starts to thicken. Remove from heat and set aside.

SALMON WITH CHINESE EGGPLANTS AND BEAN SPROUTS

Preheat your oven to 375°F. Place the oil in a cast-iron skillet and warm over medium-high heat. Add the eggplants, bell pepper, and scallion whites to the pan and cook for 5 minutes while stirring occasionally. Add your bean sprouts and stir until all the vegetables are evenly coated by the oil.

Place the salmon on the vegetables, flesh side up, season with salt, pepper, and teriyaki sauce, and transfer the pan to the oven. Cook for 8 to 10 minutes, remove pan from the oven, top with more teriyaki sauce, and serve.

SKILLET PIZZA

YIELD: *4 TO 6 SERVINGS*	**ACTIVE TIME:** *10 MINUTES*	**START TO FINISH:** *25 TO 30 MINUTES*

Surviving on frozen pizza? This recipe will break you out of the Ice Age. The key is preheating your skillet in the oven while you prepare the dough to ensure a crispy crust.

10 OZ. BALL OF PIZZA DOUGH

¼ CUP FLOUR

⅛ CUP SEMOLINA FLOUR
   OR COARSELY GROUND
   CORNMEAL

1 CUP TOMATO SAUCE

2 TO 3 CUPS MOZZARELLA

SALT AND PEPPER TO TASTE

PREFERRED TOPPINGS
   (OPTIONAL)

Place the cast-iron skillet in the oven and preheat to the highest available temperature.

Sprinkle a work surface with half of the flour. Place the pizza dough on the work surface and sprinkle the remaining flour on the dough. Working with your hands, press the dough into an even layer. Use a rolling pin to roll the dough until it is ¼ inch thick and large enough to fill the skillet.

Use oven mitts to remove the skillet from the oven. Sprinkle the semolina flour or cornmeal on the bottom of the pan. Transfer the dough to the skillet and press it into an even layer with your fingers. Spread the sauce on the dough, then sprinkle the mozzarella on top. Return the skillet to the oven and cook for 12 to 15 minutes, or until the crust is golden brown and the cheese is bubbling.

Tips: If you don't make your own dough, there are good pre-made options at the grocery store. You can also run down to the local pizza joint and ask to purchase a ball of dough.

For a simple, tasty sauce, combine a 28 oz. can of pureed San Marzano tomatoes, 1 teaspoon of sea salt, and 2 tablespoons of extra virgin olive oil.

FIVE-ONION SOUP

YIELD: *4 TO 6 SERVINGS*	**ACTIVE TIME:** *30 MINUTES*	**START TO FINISH:** *2 HOURS*

*We tend to think of the fall and winter as the only seasons for soup,
but this one should be a staple all year long. If you enjoy
a nice, cold stout, here's a perfect opportunity to crack one open.*

1 POUND WHITE ONIONS, PEELED AND SLICED THIN

1 POUND YELLOW ONIONS, PEELED AND SLICED THIN

1 POUND VIDALIA ONIONS, PEELED AND SLICED THIN

½ POUND CIPOLLINI ONIONS, PEELED AND SLICED THIN

½ POUND SHALLOTS, PEELED AND SLICED THIN

3 GARLIC CLOVES, SLICED THIN

8 TABLESPOONS SALTED BUTTER, PLUS 6 TABLESPOONS, SOFTENED

¼ CUP FLOUR

½ CUP RED WINE (BURGUNDY IS RECOMMENDED)

2 TABLESPOONS FRESH THYME LEAVES

8 CUPS BEEF STOCK

1 TABLESPOON DARK SOY SAUCE

2 BAY LEAVES

SALT AND PEPPER TO TASTE

6 PIECES OF SOURDOUGH BREAD, 1 INCH THICK

12 SLICES OF SWISS CHEESE

Place the onions, shallots, garlic, and the 8 tablespoons of butter in a cast-iron pan and cook over medium heat until the onions get a rich, caramel color, about 30 to 40 minutes.

Add the flour and stir until incorporated. Add the red wine to deglaze the pan, making sure to scrape the bottom with a wooden spoon to remove any bits that have started to stick. Add the thyme, beef stock, soy sauce, bay leaves, salt, and pepper. Reduce the heat so that the soup gently simmers, and cook until the broth lightly coats a spoon.

When the soup is close to finished, preheat your broiler and spread the softened butter on the sourdough bread. Place the bread in the oven and toast until brown and crispy, about 5 minutes. Remove from the oven and set aside.

Ladle the soup into bowls and top each one with 1 piece of toast and 2 slices of cheese. Place the bowls under the broiler until the cheese is melted and bubbly.

Tips: A quick way to peel cipollini onions is to submerge them in boiling water for a few minutes to loosen the skins. Then remove the tops and bottoms with a small knife and squeeze the onions out.

If you want to make this soup vegetarian, use vegetable stock and add another tablespoon of dark soy sauce.

APPLE AND PEAR CRUMBLE

| **YIELD:** *4 TO 6 SERVINGS* | **ACTIVE TIME:** *30 MINUTES* | **START TO FINISH:** *1 HOUR AND 15 MINUTES* |

The tart pop of the Granny Smith apples and the sweet softness of the red pears give this dish a wonderful balance. Adding freshly grated ginger to the topping really sets this one apart.

TOPPING

½ CUP WHOLE WHEAT FLOUR

1 STICK UNSALTED BUTTER, CUT INTO SMALL PIECES

½ CUP OATS

½ CUP BROWN SUGAR

¼ CUP WHITE SUGAR

1 TABLESPOON FRESH GRATED GINGER

½ TEASPOON CINNAMON

½ TEASPOON NUTMEG

½ TEASPOON KOSHER SALT

APPLE AND PEAR CRUMBLE

2 TABLESPOONS UNSALTED BUTTER

PINCH OF KOSHER SALT

2 TABLESPOONS BROWN SUGAR

2 TABLESPOONS TAPIOCA STARCH OR CORNSTARCH

3 GRANNY SMITH APPLES, EACH PEELED, QUARTERED, AND CUT INTO 20 EVEN SLICES

3 RED PEARS, EACH PEELED, QUARTERED, AND CUT INTO 16 EVEN SLICES

1 TABLESPOON VANILLA EXTRACT

1 TABLESPOON ALMOND EXTRACT

JUICE OF ½ A LEMON

TOPPING

Place all of the ingredients in a large mixing bowl and use a fork to mash the butter and other ingredients together. Continue until the topping is a collection of pea-sized pieces. Place the bowl in the refrigerator.

APPLE AND PEAR CRUMBLE

Preheat the oven to 350°F.

Place an 8-inch cast-iron skillet over medium heat. Add the butter. Place the salt, brown sugar, and tapioca starch or cornstarch in a bowl and stir to combine.

Once the butter has melted, put the apple slices in the pan in one even layer, working from the outside toward the center. Cook for 5 to 7 minutes.

Sprinkle half of the brown sugar-and-salt mixture on top of the apples.

Using the same technique you used for the apple slices, layer all of the pear slices in the skillet. Sprinkle the remaining brown sugar-and-salt mixture on top. Top with the remaining apple slices.

Combine the vanilla extract, almond extract, and lemon juice in a bowl and pour over all of the fruit.

Remove the topping from the fridge and spread in an even layer on top of the fruit. Cover the skillet with foil and cook for 15 minutes.

Remove the foil and cook for another 20 minutes.

If you would like the crisp to set, turn the oven off and open the door slightly. Let the skillet rest in the oven for another 20 minutes. Remove the skillet, top the crisp with your favorite ice cream or whipped cream, and serve.

DUTCH OVEN

Searing? Stewing? Frying? The Dutch oven can easily handle almost anything you throw at it. Traditionally used while cooking over an open flame, the Dutch oven shines in lengthy preparations where its superior heat-conducting capability allows for long simmering. A quality one can be a little pricey, but if you're feeling guilty after picking one up, make the Chicken Legs with Potatoes and Fennel (see page 150) and you'll see that it was well worth the investment.

SPAGHETTI AND MEATBALLS

YIELD: *4 TO 6 SERVINGS*	**ACTIVE TIME:** *30 MINUTES*	**START TO FINISH:** *3 HOURS*

You can't miss with these meatballs, whether you put them over pasta, in a sub, or on their own with a little sauce and cheese.

1 POUND SPAGHETTI OR
  LINGUINE NOODLES

4 TABLESPOONS EXTRA VIRGIN
  OLIVE OIL

2 GARLIC CLOVES, MINCED

1 WHITE ONION, MINCED

⅛ CUP FLAT-LEAF PARSLEY,
  CHOPPED

1 POUND GROUND BEEF
  (85% LEAN)

1 POUND GROUND PORK

1 POUND GROUND VEAL

1 CUP LIGHT CREAM

5-INCH SECTION OF ITALIAN
  BREAD, CRUST REMOVED,
  MINCED

2 EGGS

¾ CUP PARMESAN CHEESE,
  GRATED

1 TABLESPOON BASIL, MINCED

1 TABLESPOON SALT, PLUS
  MORE FOR SEASONING

BLACK PEPPER TO TASTE

6 CUPS SLOW MARINARA
  (SEE RECIPE 87)

LOAF OF GARLIC BREAD, SLICED

Fill the Dutch oven with water. Add a tablespoon of salt and bring to a boil. Add the pasta and cook for 7 to 10 minutes or until al dente. Drain and transfer the pasta to a bowl. Add 2 tablespoons of the olive oil, toss to coat, and set aside.

Place a Dutch oven over high heat and add the remaining olive oil.

Add the garlic, onion, and parsley and cook for 7 to 10 minutes, or until the onions start to caramelize. Remove the mixture from the pot and let cool.

When the onion-and-garlic mixture has cooled, place it in a bowl with all of the meat, the cream, bread pieces, eggs, Parmesan, and basil. Season with salt and pepper and gently stir to combine. Make sure not to overwork the mixture or the meatballs could get a little tough. Place a small piece of the mixture in the Dutch oven and cook until it is cooked through. Taste and adjust seasoning if necessary. Then form the remaining mixture into meatballs.

Place half of the meatballs in the Dutch oven and cook over medium-high heat for 3 minutes. Gently flip with a flexible spatula and cook for 3 minutes. Repeat with the remaining meatballs. Once all the meatballs are seared, remove and set on a plate lined with a paper towel to drain. Drain any grease from the Dutch oven and wipe clean.

Place the marinara in the Dutch oven and cook over medium-low heat. Add the meatballs, cover the pot, and cook for 2 to 2½ hours. Gently stir the sauce every 30 minutes to make sure that it does not burn.

When the sauce is nearly done cooking, add the pasta to the Dutch oven and stir until heated through. Serve with garlic bread on the side.

SHEPHERD'S PIE

YIELD: *4 TO 6 SERVINGS*	**ACTIVE TIME:** *15 MINUTES*	**START TO FINISH:** *60 TO 90 MINUTES*

This simple dish was one of my favorites as a child.
While my palate has matured, I've still got a soft spot for it.

¾ POUND LAMB

¼ POUND GROUND BEEF (85% LEAN)

1½ CUPS WHITE ONIONS, DICED

2 POUNDS RED POTATOES, DICED

2 POUNDS YELLOW POTATOES, DICED

1 TABLESPOON SALT, PLUS MORE TO TASTE

1 STICK OF BUTTER

1 CUP HALF-AND-HALF

3 TABLESPOONS BLACK TRUFFLES, MINCED

1 CUP FLOUR

4 CUPS BEEF STOCK

2 CUPS PEAS (FRESH WHEN POSSIBLE)

1 CUP CORN (FRESH WHEN POSSIBLE)

1 TABLESPOON DARK SOY SAUCE

1 TABLESPOON WORCESTERSHIRE SAUCE

Preheat oven to 350°F. Place the lamb and beef in a Dutch oven and cook over medium-high heat until brown, about 10 minutes. Drain off the fat, transfer the meat to a bowl, and set aside. Add the onions, cook until translucent, and then add to the bowl containing the meat.

Wipe out the Dutch oven and add the potatoes and the tablespoon of salt. Cover with water, bring to a boil, and cook until soft. Drain, return the potatoes to the Dutch oven, and add the butter, half-and-half, and the truffles. Season with salt and mash the potatoes until they are smooth. Set aside.

Place the Dutch oven over medium-high heat and add the meat, onions, and flour. Cook, stirring constantly for 5 minutes. Add the beef stock, peas, corn, soy sauce, and Worcestershire sauce and cook for 10 to 15 minutes while stirring.

Place the mashed potatoes on top and transfer the Dutch oven to the oven. Bake for 20 minutes until the "pie" is hot in the center.

Tip: Truffles are not an easy ingredient to find, but they will bring this dish to the next level. If you cannot find black truffles, use half of the amount of butter and substitute with that amount of truffle oil, which you can find at most specialty grocery stores.

KEFTA WITH WARM CHICKPEAS AND SALAD

YIELD: *4 TO 6 SERVINGS*	**ACTIVE TIME:** *30 TO 35 MINUTES*	**START TO FINISH:** *24 HOURS*

Think of Kefta as a Moroccan meatball with the lemon zest lending a welcome brightness to these typically earthy elements.

KEFTA

1 POUND GROUND BEEF (85% LEAN RECOMMENDED)

1 POUND GROUND LAMB

½ CUP WHITE ONION, MINCED

2 GARLIC CLOVES, ROASTED AND MASHED

ZEST OF 1 LEMON

1 CUP PARSLEY, WASHED AND MINCED

2 TABLESPOONS MINT

1 TEASPOON CINNAMON

2 TABLESPOONS CUMIN

1 TABLESPOON PAPRIKA

1 TEASPOON GROUND CORIANDER

SALT AND PEPPER TO TASTE (BE A LITTLE MORE LIBERAL WITH THE SALT)

¼ CUP OLIVE OIL

6 WOODEN SKEWERS

Continued...

KEFTA

In a mixing bowl, add all ingredients except for the olive oil and stir until well combined. Cook a small bit of the mixture as a test and taste. Adjust seasoning as necessary. Then form the mixture into 18 ovals. Place three meatballs on each skewer. Add the olive oil to a Dutch oven and warm over medium-high heat. Working in batches, add three skewers to the pot and sear the Kefta for 2 minutes on each side. Set aside.

Return the skewers to the pot, cover, and remove it from heat. Let stand for 10 minutes so the Kefta get cooked through.

When the Kefta are cooked through, remove the skewers and set aside. Place the chickpeas and salad on your serving plates, top with the Kefta, and serve.

CHICKPEAS

Add all of the ingredients to the Dutch oven and reduce the heat to medium. Cover and cook for 1 hour. Remove cover, check the beans for doneness, and raise the heat to medium-high. Cook for an additional 30 minutes, or until approximately 85% of the liquid has evaporated.

SALAD

Place all ingredients in a small mixing bowl and stir until combined.

CHICKPEAS

½ CUP GARBANZO BEANS, SOAKED
    OVERNIGHT

4 CUPS CHICKEN STOCK

½ ONION, DICED

½ CUP CILANTRO STEMS, MINCED

2 TABLESPOONS EXTRA VIRGIN
    OLIVE OIL

JUICE OF 1 LEMON

¼ TEASPOON SAFFRON

1 TABLESPOON CUMIN

1 TEASPOON CINNAMON

½ TEASPOON CRUSHED RED
    PEPPER FLAKES

SALT AND PEPPER TO TASTE

SALAD

1 LARGE TOMATO, CUT INTO
    ½-INCH THICK SLICES

1 ENGLISH CUCUMBER, SEEDS
    REMOVED, CUT INTO ½-INCH
    THICK SLICES

½ CUP PARSLEY, CHOPPED

JUICE OF ½ A LEMON

DOLLOP OF SOUR CREAM OR
    GREEK YOGURT

2 TO 3 TABLESPOONS PRESERVED
    LEMON RIND, MINCED, FOR
    GARNISH (OPTIONAL)

SALT AND PEPPER TO TASTE

THICK-CUT PORK CHOPS WITH STONE FRUIT AND BULGUR WHEAT

YIELD: *4 SERVINGS*	**ACTIVE TIME:** *15 TO 25 MINUTES*	**START TO FINISH:** *40 MINUTES*

Pork is the perfect vehicle for stone fruit, as its slightly salty flavor allows the fruit's natural sweetness to shine.

2 CUPS CHICKEN STOCK

1 CUP BULGUR WHEAT

1 TEASPOON SALT, PLUS MORE TO TASTE

ZEST OF 1 LEMON

¼ TEASPOON CRACKED BLACK PEPPER, PLUS MORE TO TASTE

1 TABLESPOON EXTRA VIRGIN OLIVE OIL

4 TABLESPOONS CANOLA OIL (OR PREFERRED NEUTRAL OIL)

4 PIECES STONE FRUIT (NECTARINES, PEACHES, PLUMS), QUARTERED AND PITTED

1 TURNIP, PEELED AND DICED FINE

4 TO 6 CIPOLLINI ONIONS, PEELED AND HALVED LENGTHWISE

4 THICK-CUT PORK CHOPS (ABOUT 1-INCH THICK)

2 TABLESPOONS FRESH THYME LEAVES, FOR GARNISH

Place the chicken stock in the Dutch oven and bring to a boil. Place the bulgur wheat, salt, lemon zest, pepper, and olive oil in a bowl and pour the chicken stock over it. Cover tightly with plastic wrap and set aside for 30 minutes.

Preheat the oven to 375°F. Wipe out the pot, place 2 tablespoons of the cooking oil in it, and warm over medium heat. When the oil starts to glisten, place the stone fruit, flesh-side down, in the Dutch oven and sear for about 3 minutes per side. Add the diced turnip and cipollini onions and cook for about 2 minutes per side. Remove the mixture from the pot and set aside.

Season the pork chops with salt and pepper. Add the remaining cooking oil and then place the pork chops in the Dutch oven. Cook for about 5 minutes on each side until a crust starts to form and the centers of the chops are 140°F to 145°F. Remove the pork chops and set aside.

Chop the onions. Add the turnip and the onions to the bulgur wheat. Fluff with a fork and place the mixture in the Dutch oven. Arrange the fruit around the edge of the pot and place it in the oven. Cook for 5 to 7 minutes, until warmed through. Remove, divide between the serving plates, top with the pork chops, and garnish with the thyme.

Tip: If you want to know if the oil is ready or aren't sure if it is shimmering, flick a few drops of water into the oil. If the oil sizzles, it is ready.

DUTCH PEA SOUP

YIELD: *6 SERVINGS*	**ACTIVE TIME:** *30 MINUTES*	**START TO FINISH:** *3 TO 4 HOURS*

This thick soup is traditionally served around New Year's and typically features rookworst. Since this rookworst can be difficult to find outside of the Netherlands, we've switched it out for kielbasa.

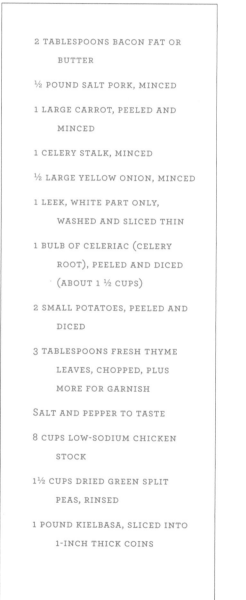

2 TABLESPOONS BACON FAT OR
BUTTER

½ POUND SALT PORK, MINCED

1 LARGE CARROT, PEELED AND
MINCED

1 CELERY STALK, MINCED

½ LARGE YELLOW ONION, MINCED

1 LEEK, WHITE PART ONLY,
WASHED AND SLICED THIN

1 BULB OF CELERIAC (CELERY
ROOT), PEELED AND DICED
(ABOUT 1 ½ CUPS)

2 SMALL POTATOES, PEELED AND
DICED

3 TABLESPOONS FRESH THYME
LEAVES, CHOPPED, PLUS
MORE FOR GARNISH

SALT AND PEPPER TO TASTE

8 CUPS LOW-SODIUM CHICKEN
STOCK

1½ CUPS DRIED GREEN SPLIT
PEAS, RINSED

1 POUND KIELBASA, SLICED INTO
1-INCH THICK COINS

Place a Dutch oven over medium-high heat and add the bacon fat or butter. Add the salt pork, carrot, celery, onion, leek, celeriac, potatoes, thyme, salt, and pepper and cook for 10 minutes, or until the vegetables start to caramelize.

Add the chicken stock and the green split peas and reduce the heat to medium-low. Cook for 2 to 2½ hours, or until the peas have broken down and your spoon can stand up in the pot. Make sure to stir the soup every 15 to 20 minutes to keep it from burning.

Top with the kielbasa, garnish with the additional thyme, and serve.

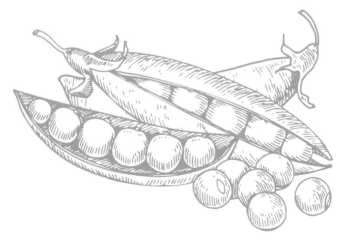

CHICKEN AND PANCETTA CASSOULET

YIELD: 6 SERVINGS	**ACTIVE TIME:** 30 TO 35 MINUTES	**START TO FINISH:** 24 HOURS

This French classic usually takes a few days to make and utilizes duck instead of chicken. This adaptation is quicker, without sacrificing any of the dish's famous flavor.

1 POUND CANNELLINI BEANS, SOAKED OVERNIGHT

8 CUPS WATER

2 TABLESPOONS BACON FAT

¼ POUND PANCETTA, MINCED

¾ POUND SAUSAGE (GARLIC SAUSAGE IS PREFERRED; A MILD ITALIAN SAUSAGE WILL WORK), DICED

6 TO 8 BONELESS, SKINLESS CHICKEN THIGHS

1 LARGE CARROT, MINCED

3 CELERY STALKS, MINCED

1 WHITE ONION, MINCED

SALT AND PEPPER TO TASTE

3 TO 4 LARGE GARLIC CLOVES, ROASTED

3 ROMA TOMATOES, DICED

6 TO 8 SPRIGS OF FRESH THYME, LEAVES REMOVED

¼ CUP PARSLEY, PLUS MORE FOR GARNISH

½ TABLESPOON WHOLE CLOVES

3 TO 4 BAY LEAVES

¼ CUP WHITE WINE

4 CUPS LOW-SODIUM CHICKEN STOCK

Place the beans and the water in a Dutch oven and cook until the beans are almost cooked through, about 50 minutes. Drain and set the beans aside.

Place the Dutch oven over medium-high heat and add the bacon fat and the pancetta. Cook for 5 minutes and then add the sausage. Cook the sausage for 7 to 10 minutes, or until the fat has been rendered and the meat is slightly crispy.

Using a slotted spoon, remove the pancetta and sausage from the pot. Season the chicken thighs with salt and pepper, place them in the pot, and sear for 5 minutes per side. Remove the chicken from the pot and set aside.

Add the carrot, celery, and onion to the Dutch oven. Season with salt and pepper and cook, stirring occasionally, until the vegetables start to caramelize, about 10 to 12 minutes.

Place the roasted garlic, tomatoes, thyme, parsley, cloves, and bay leaves in the pot. Stir and cook for 5 minutes. Deglaze the pot with the white wine and use a wooden spoon to scrape the browned bits from the bottom of the pot. Cook for 3 minutes.

Return the chicken, pancetta, sausage, and beans to the Dutch oven. Add the chicken stock, reduce the heat to medium-low or low, cover, and cook for 2 to 3 hours, checking every half-hour for doneness. The dish is done when almost all of the stock is gone.

Remove lid, discard the bay leaves, garnish with additional parsley, and serve.

Tip: If you want to roast garlic at home, all you need is 1 head of garlic. Remove the top just enough to see the cloves inside their skins, preheat the oven to 375°F, and place the head of garlic, cut-side up, in a square of aluminum foil. Drizzle the garlic with olive oil, place a pat of butter on top, and close the foil over the garlic. Place in the oven and roast for 45 minutes to 1 hour. The garlic cloves should look slightly brown, be extremely fragrant, and be easy to squeeze from their skins.

CHICKEN TORTILLA SOUP

YIELD: *4 TO 6 SERVINGS*	**ACTIVE TIME:** *30 MINUTES*	**START TO FINISH:** *1 HOUR AND 30 MINUTES*

The secret weapon in this soup is the hint of adobo sauce. Make sure you use chicken thighs, as they are perfect for shredding and won't dry out.

8 CORN TORTILLAS

3 TABLESPOONS CANOLA OIL (OR
    PREFERRED NEUTRAL OIL)

2 TABLESPOONS GARLIC, MINCED

6 BONELESS, SKINLESS CHICKEN
    THIGHS

½ LARGE YELLOW ONION, DICED

1 POBLANO PEPPER, SEEDED AND
    DICED

1 ANAHEIM PEPPER, SEEDED AND
    DICED

4 PLUM TOMATOES, DICED

2 TABLESPOONS ADOBO SAUCE
    FROM A CAN OF CHIPOTLES
    IN ADOBO

1 TABLESPOON CUMIN

2 DRIED ARBOL CHILIES, SEEDED
    AND MINCED

4 CUPS CHICKEN STOCK

1 CUP WATER

2 TABLESPOONS KOSHER SALT,
    PLUS MORE FOR SEASONING

COTIJA CHEESE, FOR GARNISH

CILANTRO, CHOPPED, FOR
    GARNISH

Preheat the oven to 375°F. Cut six of the tortillas into small strips and set two aside.

Line a baking sheet with parchment paper and place the tortilla strips on the sheet. Brush the strips with 1 tablespoon of the oil and then sprinkle them with kosher salt. Place the sheet in the oven and bake for 15 to 20 minutes, or until they become crispy. Remove from the oven and set aside.

Place the remaining oil and the garlic in the Dutch oven and cook over medium-high heat until the oil and garlic become fragrant, about 5 minutes.

Add the chicken to the pot and sear for 5 minutes on each side. Remove the chicken from the pot and set aside. The chicken should still be slightly undercooked.

Place the onion, peppers, tomatoes, adobo sauce, cumin, and chilies in the pot and cook for 10 to 15 minutes, stirring the mixture every couple of minutes.

Return the chicken to the pan. Add the 2 tablespoons of kosher salt, chicken stock, and water and cook for 1 hour or until the chicken shreds easily when pressed against the side of the pot with a wooden spoon.

Add the reserved whole tortillas and continue cooking until they dissolve, about 10 minutes. Garnish with Cotija cheese, cilantro, and your crispy tortilla strips.

Tip: If you don't want to turn on the oven, you can use your favorite kind of corn chips in place of the crispy tortillas.

TUSCAN CHICKEN AND WHITE BEAN STEW

YIELD: *4 TO 6 SERVINGS*	**ACTIVE TIME:** *30 TO 45 MINUTES*	**START TO FINISH:** *1 HOUR AND 45 MINUTES*

*The pureed beans provide the same rich texture
as cream without any of the heaviness.*

1 POUND CANNELLINI BEANS, SOAKED

2 POUNDS CHICKEN THIGHS, BONED
AND SKINNED, BONES RESERVED

2 BAY LEAVES

1 TABLESPOON KOSHER SALT

2 SPRIGS OF ROSEMARY

SALT AND PEPPER TO TASTE

2 TABLESPOONS EXTRA VIRGIN OLIVE
OIL, PLUS MORE FOR DRIZZLING

1 YELLOW ONION, PEELED AND DICED

3 CARROTS, DICED

2 CELERY STALKS, DICED

1 YELLOW BELL PEPPER, SEEDED AND
DICED

1 ORANGE BELL PEPPER, SEEDED AND
DICED

3 GARLIC CLOVES, MINCED

1 TEASPOON CRUSHED RED PEPPER
FLAKES

4 SMALL ROMA TOMATOES, DICED

2 TABLESPOONS FRESH SAGE, CHOPPED

1½ OZ. ASIAGO CHEESE, GRATED

¼ CUP FRESH BASIL, CHOPPED

SCALLIONS, CHOPPED, FOR GARNISH

Drain the cannellini beans and rinse them. Place in the Dutch oven, cover with water, and cook over medium heat. Add the chicken bones, bay leaves, kosher salt, and the rosemary. Cover and cook, stirring occasionally for about 1 hour, until the beans are soft and starting to fall apart.

While the beans are cooking, season the chicken with salt and pepper and set aside.

When the beans are done, pour them into a bowl. Remove the chicken bones, rosemary sprigs, and the bay leaves. Place the Dutch oven back on the stove and add the olive oil. Warm over medium heat and then add the chicken thighs. Cook for about 5 minutes on each side until the chicken is cooked through. Remove from the pot and let cool. When cool, dice the chicken.

Place the onion, carrots, celery, peppers, garlic, crushed red pepper flakes, tomatoes, and sage in the pot and cook for 20 minutes until the vegetables are soft and have released their juices. While the vegetables are cooking, transfer the beans to a blender and puree. Place the beans back in the pot and then stir in the Asiago and basil. Season with salt and pepper and cook for 7 to 10 minutes until the cheese is melted. Return the diced chicken to the pot and cook until heated through. Drizzle with additional olive oil, garnish with scallions if desired, and serve.

Tip: If you don't want to use a blender, you can mash the beans by hand until they are smooth.

CHICKEN LEGS WITH POTATOES AND FENNEL

YIELD: 6 SERVINGS	ACTIVE TIME: 30 MINUTES	START TO FINISH: 1 HOUR AND 10 MINUTES

This meal takes me back to my grandmother's kitchen, where I often sat and watched her cook. Turn to this one when you need some comfort; it's likely to stick with you for a while.

⅓ CUP OLIVE OIL, PLUS 2 TABLESPOONS

6 CHICKEN LEGS, SKIN ON

½ CUP SHALLOTS, MINCED

1½ TABLESPOONS GARLIC, MINCED

2 RED POTATOES, DICED

3 TO 4 YELLOW POTATOES, DICED

3 FENNEL BULBS, DICED, FRONDS RESERVED FOR GARNISH

1 TABLESPOON KOSHER SALT, PLUS MORE TO TASTE

1 TABLESPOON CRACKED BLACK PEPPER, PLUS MORE TO TASTE

1 TEASPOON CELERY SEEDS

1 TEASPOON FENNEL SEEDS

½ CUP SUN-DRIED TOMATOES

1 CUP CHARDONNAY

6 TABLESPOONS SALTED BUTTER

Place the Dutch oven over medium-high heat and add ⅓ cup of the olive oil. While the oil heats up, rub the chicken legs with the remaining oil and season with the salt and pepper. When the oil is hot, add half of the chicken, skin side down, and cook until the skin is golden brown and crusted. Remove, set aside, and repeat with the remaining chicken legs.

Preheat the oven to 400°F. Add the shallots and garlic to the Dutch oven and use a wooden spoon to scrape all of the browned bits from the bottom. Cook until the shallots and garlic darken, about 3 minutes.

Turn the heat up to high and add the remaining ingredients, besides the Chardonnay and the butter. Cook for about 15 minutes while stirring every few minutes.

Add the wine and the butter, stir, and then return the chicken to the pot, skin-side up. Reduce the heat, cover, and cook until the potatoes are soft and the chicken is 155°F in the center. Remove the lid, transfer the Dutch oven to the oven, and cook until the chicken is 165°F in the center. Garnish with the fennel fronds and serve.

Tip: To check the temperature of the chicken, insert a kitchen thermometer at the fattest point, next to the bone. I suggest a digital thermometer for ease of use. To calibrate the thermometer, submerge the tip in a cup of ice water. It should read 32°F.

CHICKEN AND VEGETABLE STEW

YIELD: *6 SERVINGS*	ACTIVE TIME: *15 TO 20 MINUTES*	START TO FINISH: *1 HOUR AND 45 MINUTES*

If you're going to make this stew, make sure you use the recipe for homemade chicken stock. The flavor it adds is essential.

2 TABLESPOONS OLIVE OIL

2 POUNDS CHICKEN THIGHS

SALT AND PEPPER TO TASTE

1 WHITE ONION, DICED

3 CELERY STALKS, DICED

2 CARROTS, DICED

2 PARSNIPS, DICED

1 ZUCCHINI, DICED

1 YELLOW SQUASH, DICED

3 GARLIC CLOVES, MINCED

8 CUPS CHICKEN STOCK [SEE RECIPE PAGE 154)

2 BAY LEAVES

FRESH BASIL, CHOPPED, FOR GARNISH (OPTIONAL)

Place the olive oil in a Dutch oven and warm over medium-high heat. Season the chicken thighs with salt and pepper and place them in the Dutch oven, skin side down. Cook for 5 minutes on each side. Remove and set aside.

Add the onion, celery, carrots, and parsnips to the pot and cook for 5 to 7 minutes, until the onion starts to get translucent. Season with a pinch of salt and pepper and then add the zucchini, squash, and garlic. Cook for 5 minutes while stirring until the garlic is fragrant.

Season with salt and pepper and add the chicken thighs, chicken stock, and bay leaves. Reduce heat to medium, cover, and cook for 1½ hours or until the chicken is falling off the bone. Season with salt and pepper to taste. Discard the bay leaves and, if desired, garnish with fresh basil before serving.

Tip: Since you're going to need a chicken carcass for the stock, one option is to spatchcock a chicken (see page 205), remove the meat for the stew, and use the bones for the stock.

CHICKEN STOCK

| YIELD: *4 CUPS* | ACTIVE TIME: *15 MINUTES* | START TO FINISH: *12 TO 16 HOURS* |

Homemade chicken stock will always be better than store-bought versions. Whip this up and see if you agree.

BONES FROM 1 WHOLE CHICKEN

1 ONION, CHOPPED

2 CARROTS, CUT INTO 2-INCH
PIECES

3 CELERY STALKS

1 BUNCH OF PARSLEY STEMS,
LEAVES REMOVED

2 BAY LEAVES

2 TABLESPOONS BLACK
PEPPERCORNS

8 CUPS WATER

SALT TO TASTE

Place all of the ingredients in a crock-pot, cover, and cook on low for a minimum of 12 hours. The longer the stock cooks, the richer the flavor will be. If you're going to cook it for longer than 12 hours, add another cup of water.

Strain, discard solids, and transfer the stock to the refrigerator. When it has cooled, remove the layer of fat from the top.

PUERTO RICAN RICE AND BEANS

YIELD: *6 SERVINGS* | **ACTIVE TIME:** *15 MINUTES* | **START TO FINISH:** *1 HOUR AND 45 MINUTES*

This one comes from my daughter's great-grandmother, who hails from Puerto Rico. After watching it prepared countless times, I finally pinned down a recipe. Now, I prepare it any time there's a family gathering.

½ POUND KIDNEY BEANS, SOAKED OVERNIGHT AND DRAINED

½ CUP VEGETABLE OIL

4 BONELESS, SKINLESS CHICKEN THIGHS

2 PIECES SALT PORK, MINCED (ABOUT ½ CUP)

1 CUP SOFRITO (SEE PAGE 44)

1 CUP OF SPANISH-STYLE TOMATO SAUCE, PUREED

2 CUPS WHITE RICE

3 TO 3½ CUPS CHICKEN STOCK

2 PACKETS OF SAZÓN WITH ACHIOTE

2 TABLESPOONS DRIED OREGANO

1 CUP SPANISH OLIVES WITH THE BRINE

ADOBO SEASONING TO TASTE

Place the beans in a Dutch oven and cover with water. Bring to a boil, reduce heat to medium-low, and cover the pot. Cook for 45 minutes to 1 hour, until the beans are tender. Drain and set the beans aside.

Place the pot back on the stove and add ¼ cup of the oil. Add the chicken and cook over medium-high heat for 5 minutes on each side. Remove the chicken from the Dutch oven, cut it into 12 pieces, and set aside.

Add the salt pork and the remaining oil to the pot and cook until some of the salt pork's fat has rendered, about 5 minutes. Add the Sofrito and the tomato sauce. Cook for 5 minutes, stirring constantly.

Add the rice to the pot, stir, and cook for 5 minutes. Add the remaining ingredients and return the chicken to the pot. Reduce heat to medium and cook for 10 minutes. Cover the Dutch oven and cook for another 20 to 30 minutes, or until the liquid has been absorbed and the rice is tender.

Uncover the pot and add the beans. Stir to combine and serve.

Tip: The rice at the bottom of the Dutch oven might get a little crunchy. That is actually preferred for this dish.

WHITE CHICKEN CHILI

YIELD: *6 SERVINGS*	**ACTIVE TIME:** *15 MINUTES*	**START TO FINISH:** *24 HOURS*

You want the heat to be subtle in this chili to showcase the flavors of the green chilies and Sofrito. If you want to make this one special, use the recipe for Chicken Stock on page 154.

1 POUND WHITE BEANS, SOAKED OVERNIGHT AND DRAINED

¼ CUP VEGETABLE OIL

6 BONELESS, SKINLESS CHICKEN THIGHS

1 MEDIUM WHITE ONION, MINCED

3 GARLIC CLOVES, MINCED

1 CUP SOFRITO (SEE PAGE 44)

1 (7 OZ.) CAN DICED, MILD GREEN CHILIES

6 CUPS CHICKEN STOCK

1 TABLESPOON WHITE PEPPER

3 TABLESPOONS DRIED OREGANO

1 TABLESPOON CUMIN

1 TABLESPOON ADOBO SEASONING

SALT AND PEPPER TO TASTE

Place the beans in a Dutch oven and cover with water. Bring to a boil, reduce heat to medium-low, and cover the pot. Cook for 45 minutes to 1 hour until the beans are tender. Drain and set the beans aside.

Place the pot back on the stove and warm the oil over medium-high heat. Add the chicken and cook for 5 minutes on each side. Remove the chicken and set aside.

Add the onion and garlic to the pot and cook until the onions are translucent, about 5 to 7 minutes.

Add the Sofrito and green chilies and cook, stirring occasionally, for 5 minutes.

Return the beans and the chicken to the Dutch oven. Add the remaining ingredients, reduce the heat to medium, cover, and cook for 1 hour.

Remove the cover, stir, and cook for an additional 30 minutes to 1 hour, until the chili has thickened and the chicken is falling apart.

Tip: If you want to roast your own green chilies, turn your broiler on. Place fresh green chilies on a baking sheet and coat them with vegetable oil. Place the sheet in the oven and cook until the skins of the chilies are charred, about 15 to 20 minutes. Remove the sheet from the oven and place the chilies in a bowl. Cover the bowl tightly with plastic wrap and set aside. After 30 minutes, use your fingers to remove the charred skins of the peppers. Dice the chilies and reserve until ready to use.

JAMBALAYA

YIELD: *4 TO 6 SERVINGS*	**ACTIVE TIME:** *25 MINUTES*	**START TO FINISH:** *1 HOUR AND 15 MINUTES*

Charring the sausages at the beginning of your preparation adds an indispensable smokiness to this Cajun classic.

½ POUND ANDOUILLE SAUSAGE, CUT INTO ½-INCH THICK COINS

½ POUND SHRIMP (21/25), SHELLED AND DEVEINED

¼ CUP VEGETABLE OIL

4 BONELESS, SKINLESS CHICKEN THIGHS OR BREASTS, CUT INTO 2-INCH CUBES

1 LARGE YELLOW ONION, DICED

1 LARGE GREEN OR RED BELL PEPPER, DICED

2 CELERY STALKS, DICED (ABOUT 1 CUP)

3 GARLIC CLOVES, MINCED

2 TO 3 PLUM TOMATOES, DICED

2 BAY LEAVES

2 TABLESPOONS PAPRIKA

2 TABLESPOONS DRIED THYME

1 TABLESPOON GRANULATED GARLIC

1 TABLESPOON GRANULATED ONION

1 TEASPOON CAYENNE PEPPER

1½ CUPS LONG-GRAIN WHITE RICE

2 TABLESPOONS WORCESTERSHIRE SAUCE

TABASCO TO TASTE

3 CUPS CHICKEN STOCK

SALT AND PEPPER TO TASTE

SCALLIONS, CHOPPED, FOR GARNISH

Place the sausage in a Dutch oven and cook over medium-high heat. Cook for 2 minutes on each side, remove, and set aside.

Add the shrimp and cook for 1 minute on each side. Remove and set aside.

Add the oil, chicken, onion, pepper, and celery. Cook for 5 to 7 minutes, or until the vegetables start to caramelize and the chicken is cooked through. Add the garlic and cook for another 2 minutes.

Add the tomatoes, bay leaves, and all of the spices. Cook for 30 minutes, stirring occasionally to prevent the contents of the Dutch oven from burning.

Add the rice, Worcestershire sauce, Tabasco, and chicken stock. Return the sausage to the pot, reduce heat to medium-low, cover, and cook for 25 minutes.

Return the shrimp to the pot, cover, and cook for 5 minutes. Ladle into bowls and garnish with scallions.

LOBSTER CIOPPINO

YIELD: *6 SERVINGS*	**ACTIVE TIME:** *30 TO 40 MINUTES*	**START TO FINISH:** *1 HOUR AND 30 MINUTES*

This fisherman's stew originated in San Francisco, but since I come from the land of lobster, I decided to inject a bit of New England into this version.

1 (1¼-POUND) LOBSTER

1 POUND PEI MUSSELS, WASHED AND DEBEARDED

12 LITTLE NECK CLAMS, WASHED AND SCRUBBED

2 TABLESPOONS EXTRA VIRGIN OLIVE OIL

½ LARGE FENNEL BULB, SLICED THIN

2 SHALLOTS, MINCED

3 GARLIC CLOVES, MINCED

1 (6 OZ.) CAN TOMATO PASTE

1 CUP RED WINE (ZINFANDEL PREFERRED)

1 (28 OZ.) CAN WHOLE SAN MARZANO TOMATOES, LIGHTLY CRUSHED BY HAND

1 CUP WHITE WINE (CHARDONNAY PREFERRED)

2 CUPS FISH STOCK

2 BAY LEAVES

1 TEASPOON CRUSHED RED PEPPER FLAKES

1 POUND HALIBUT, SKINNED AND CUT INTO LARGE CUBES

SALT AND PEPPER TO TASTE

1 LOAF OF SOURDOUGH OR CRUSTY ITALIAN BREAD, TO SERVE

Place 3 inches of water in a Dutch oven and bring to a boil. Place the lobster in the pot, cover, and cook for 5 to 7 minutes, until the shell is a bright, reddish orange. Remove the lobster from the pot and set aside. Drain the cooking liquid and return the Dutch oven to the stove.

Add 2 cups of water and bring to a boil. Add your cleaned mussels and clams, cover the pot, and cook for 3 to 5 minutes, until the majority of the shells have opened. Drain, set aside the clams and mussels, and reserve the liquid. Discard any clams and mussels that do not open.

Place the Dutch oven over medium-high heat and add the olive oil. When the oil is warm, add the fennel and cook for 3 minutes until the fennel is soft and slightly translucent.

Add the shallots and garlic. Stir and cook for 5 minutes.

Add the tomato paste and stir to incorporate. Add the red wine and cook until it is almost evaporated, about 5 minutes. Scrape the bottom with a wooden spoon to remove any bits that are stuck.

Add the tomatoes, white wine, fish stock, bay leaves, red pepper flakes, and a pinch of salt and pepper. Reduce the heat to medium-low, cover, and cook for 30 minutes.

While the stew is cooking, use a lobster cracker or a heavy knife to crack the lobster open. Remove the tail first. Using a towel, grab the tail where it connects to the body and twist until it detaches. Do this over a bowl to catch any juices that are released. Use the cracker or knife to crack open the shell and remove the meat. If you are using a knife, press the tail flat on a cutting board, top side down. Carefully cut down the length of the tail and remove the meat.

If using a cracker, crack each claw at the joint, then crack the top part of the claw until the shell opens. Grab the bottom piece of the claw and twist it sideways. Once loose, pull straight back to remove the shell. The cartilage should also come out with it. Remove all of the meat and discard the shells. If you are using a knife, use the flat of the knife to crack the shells open. Set the lobster meat aside.

Remove the legs from the lobster and add the remaining carcass to the pot. Uncover the pot and cook for 20 minutes.

Add the halibut to the pot and cook for 5 minutes. Add the lobster meat, clams, mussels, and the reserved cooking liquid and cook for 2 minutes. Serve with a loaf of sourdough or crusty Italian bread.

Tip: If you can't get fresh lobster, use whatever fresh fish is available. You can also purchase lobster that has been pre-cleaned if you want to avoid doing the cracking and cleaning yourself.

COCONUT-BRAISED VEGETABLES WITH HALIBUT

YIELD: *4 TO 6 SERVINGS*	**ACTIVE TIME:** *30 MINUTES*	**START TO FINISH:** *1 HOUR*

*The kale is key, as it provides a nice soft bed for
the halibut and ensures that it remains moist and full of flavor.*

4 TABLESPOONS EXTRA VIRGIN OLIVE OIL

1 YELLOW BELL PEPPER, DICED

1 RED BELL PEPPER, DICED

1 HABANERO PEPPER, PIERCED

1 LARGE OR 2 SMALL WHITE SWEET
    POTATOES

1 CUP RED CABBAGE, DICED

SALT AND PEPPER TO TASTE

3 GRAFFITI EGGPLANT, CUT INTO 2-INCH
    PIECES

2 TABLESPOONS FRESH GINGER, PEELED
    AND MASHED INTO A PASTE

3 TO 4 GARLIC CLOVES, MINCED

1 TO 2 TABLESPOONS GREEN CURRY PASTE

2 TO 3 BABY BOK CHOY, CHOPPED

4 CUPS FISH STOCK

1 TO 2 TABLESPOONS SWEET PAPRIKA

2 TABLESPOONS CILANTRO, WASHED AND
    CHOPPED

3 (14 OZ.) CANS COCONUT MILK

2 BUNCHES TUSCAN KALE, LEAVES
    REMOVED AND TORN INTO LARGE
    PIECES

4 TO 6 (4 OZ.) HALIBUT FILLETS

SCALLIONS, CHOPPED, FOR GARNISH

Place the oil in a Dutch oven and warm over medium-high heat. Add the bell peppers, habanero, sweet potatoes, and cabbage. Season with salt and pepper and cook for 5 to 7 minutes while stirring, or until the sweet potatoes begin to caramelize.

Add the eggplant, ginger, and garlic and cook for 10 minutes, stirring often. Add the curry paste and stir to coat all of the vegetables. Cook for 2 minutes or until the contents of the pot are fragrant.

Add the bok choy, fish stock, paprika, cilantro, and coconut milk and cook for 15 to 25 minutes, until the liquid has been reduced by ¼.

Add the kale to the Dutch oven. Place the halibut fillets on top of the kale, reduce the heat to medium, cover, and cook for about 10 minutes, or until the fish is cooked through.

Remove the cover and discard the habanero. Ladle the vegetables and the sauce into bowls and top each one with a halibut fillet. Garnish with the scallions and serve.

FISH STEW

YIELD: *4 TO 6 SERVINGS* | **ACTIVE TIME:** *20 MINUTES* | **START TO FINISH:** *1 HOUR*

Moscatel lends sweetness and nutty notes to this buttery stew. As a result, this light soup has a rich flavor.

4 TABLESPOONS BUTTER

3 CARROTS, DICED

1 LARGE VIDALIA ONION, DICED

2 YUKON GOLD POTATOES, DICED

5 CELERY STALKS, DICED

2 FENNEL BULBS, SLICED THIN, FRONDS RESERVED FOR GARNISH

3 GARLIC CLOVES, MINCED

4 TABLESPOONS FRESH THYME, MINCED

¼ CUP FLOUR

1½ CUPS MOSCATEL

4 CUPS FISH STOCK

1 POUND HAKE, SKINNED

1 POUND COD, SKINNED

1½ CUPS FAVA BEANS, SHELLED

SALT AND PEPPER TO TASTE

Place 2 tablespoons of the butter in a Dutch oven and melt over medium-high heat. Add carrots, onion, potatoes, and celery and cook for 5 to 7 minutes, or until the vegetables start to caramelize.

Add the fennel, garlic, and thyme. Cook for another 3 to 5 minutes until the fennel softens. Add the remaining butter and stir until melted.

Sprinkle the flour over the vegetables and stir until they are evenly coated. Cook for 5 minutes, stirring occasionally.

Add the Moscatel and cook for 2 minutes while stirring. Make sure to scrape any bits from the bottom of the pan to add flavor to the dish.

Reduce the heat to medium. Add the fish stock, stir, and cook for 20 minutes, or until the flavor of the flour dissipates.

Add the fish and fava beans. Season with salt and pepper, cover, and cook for 10 minutes, or until the fish is flaky. Garnish with fennel fronds and serve.

LINGUINE WITH WHITE CLAM SAUCE

YIELD: *4 TO 6 SERVINGS*	**ACTIVE TIME:** *15 TO 20 MINUTES*	**START TO FINISH:** *30 TO 40 MINUTES*

Easy, salty, and bursting with freshness, if you don't have much time and need to whip up something special, this dish won't let you down.

1 POUND LINGUINE

2 TABLESPOONS SEA SALT

½ CUP EXTRA VIRGIN OLIVE OIL

3 GARLIC CLOVES, SLICED THIN

32 LITTLE NECK CLAMS, SCRUBBED AND RINSED

1 CUP WHITE WINE

8 OZ. CLAM JUICE

1 CUP ITALIAN PARSLEY, CHOPPED

¼ CUP PARMESAN CHEESE, GRATED

SALT AND PEPPER TO TASTE

In a Dutch oven, bring 4 quarts of water to boil. Add the linguine and sea salt. Cook for 7 minutes, or until the pasta is just short of al dente. Drain, reserve ½ cup of cooking water, and set the linguine aside.

Place the Dutch oven over medium heat. Add ½ of the olive oil and the garlic to the pot and cook until the garlic starts to brown, about 2 minutes. Add the clams and wine, cover, and cook for 5 to 7 minutes, or until the majority of the clams are open. Use a slotted spoon to transfer the clams to a colander. Discard any clams that do not open.

Add the clam juice, parsley, and pasta water to the Dutch oven. Cook until the sauce starts to thicken, about 10 minutes. Remove all the clams from their shells and mince ¼ of them.

Return the linguine to the pot. Add Parmesan, season with salt and pepper, and stir until the cheese begins to melt. Fold in the clams, drizzle with the remaining olive oil, and serve.

Tip: If you do not have access to fresh clams, you can use canned whole clams. I recommend the Bar Harbor brand.

MEL'S NEW ENGLAND CLAM CHOWDER

YIELD: *6 SERVINGS*	**ACTIVE TIME:** *30 MINUTES*	**START TO FINISH:** *1 HOUR AND 30 MINUTES*

*Packed with cherrystone clams, bacon,
and potatoes, this chowder is too good to pass up.*

½ POUND BACON, MINCED

2 TABLESPOONS FRESH THYME, CHOPPED

4 CUPS CELERY, WASHED AND MINCED

4 MEDIUM SPANISH ONIONS, PEELED AND MINCED

4 TABLESPOONS UNSALTED BUTTER

6 GARLIC CLOVES, MINCED

⅓ CUP FLOUR, PLUS 1 TABLESPOON

1½ POUNDS CREAMER POTATOES, MINCED

2 CUPS OF BAR HARBOR PURE CLAM JUICE

2 TABLESPOONS WORCESTERSHIRE SAUCE

3 DASHES TABASCO

2 CUPS HEAVY CREAM

6 (6½ OZ.) CANS OF BAR HARBOR WHOLE MAINE CHERRYSTONE CLAMS, WITH JUICE

SALT AND PEPPER TO TASTE

Place the bacon in a Dutch oven and cook over medium-high heat until the bacon is crispy. Stir the bacon occasionally as it cooks. Drain the fat from the pan and add the thyme, celery, onions, butter, and garlic. Reduce the heat to medium and cook until the onions are translucent. Add the flour and mix until all the vegetables are coated. Cook for 10 minutes while stirring frequently, scraping the bottom of the pan to keep anything from burning.

Add the potatoes and clam juice and cook until potatoes are tender, about 20 minutes. Add the Worcestershire sauce and Tabasco, stir, and then add the cream. Cook until the chowder is just thick enough to coat a spoon. Add the cherrystone clams, season with salt and pepper, and cook until heated through, about 10 minutes.

MAC AND CHEESE WITH BROWN BUTTER BREAD CRUMBS

YIELD: *6 SERVINGS*	**ACTIVE TIME:** *15 MINUTES*	**START TO FINISH:** *1 HOUR*

The cheese in this dish will stick to your ribs. Reserve it for those nights when you're especially hungry and can afford to relax after the meal.

8 OZ. PASTA

7 TABLESPOONS UNSALTED BUTTER

2 CUPS BREAD CRUMBS (USE PANKO FOR AN EXTRA CRUNCHY TOP)

½ YELLOW ONION, MINCED

3 TABLESPOONS ALL-PURPOSE FLOUR

1 TABLESPOON YELLOW MUSTARD

1 TEASPOON TURMERIC

1 TEASPOON GRANULATED GARLIC

1 TEASPOON WHITE PEPPER

2 CUPS FAT-FREE HALF-AND-HALF OR LIGHT CREAM

2 CUPS WHOLE MILK

1 POUND AMERICAN CHEESE, SLICED

10 OZ. BOURSIN CHEESE

8 OZ. EXTRA SHARP CHEDDAR, SLICED

SALT AND PEPPER TO TASTE

Preheat oven to 400°F.

Fill a Dutch oven with water and bring to a boil. Add a tablespoon or 2 of salt and then add the pasta. Cook until slightly under al dente, about 6 to 7 minutes. Drain and set aside.

Place the pot over medium heat and add 3 tablespoons of the butter. Cook until the butter starts to give off a nutty smell and brown. Add the bread crumbs, stir, and cook for 4 to 5 minutes until the bread crumbs start to look like wet sand. Remove and set aside.

Wipe the Dutch oven out with a towel, place over medium-high heat, and add the onion and the remaining butter. Cook while stirring until the onion is translucent and soft, about 7 to 10 minutes. Add your flour and whisk until there are no lumps. Add the mustard, turmeric, granulated garlic, and white pepper and whisk until combined. Add the half-and-half and the milk and whisk until incorporated.

Reduce heat to medium and bring mixture to a simmer. Once you start to see small bubbles forming around the outside of the mixture, add the cheeses one at a time, whisking to combine before adding the next one. When all the cheese has been added and the mixture is smooth, cook for 10 to 15 minutes until the flour taste is gone. Return the pasta to the pot, stir, and top with the bread crumbs.

Place in the oven and bake for 10 to 15 minutes. Remove the pot from the oven and serve.

Tip: If you can't find Boursin, whisk some cream cheese and a little softened butter together.

VEGETABLE LO MEIN

YIELD: *4 TO 6 SERVINGS*	ACTIVE TIME: *15 TO 25 MINUTES*	START TO FINISH: *30 MINUTES*

This dish works either hot or cold, making it a perfect option for summertime, when a hot meal can be the last thing you want.

¼ CUP SESAME OIL

3 TABLESPOONS SOY SAUCE

2 TABLESPOONS BLACK VINEGAR

1 TABLESPOON BROWN SUGAR

3 TABLESPOONS FISH SAUCE

1 TABLESPOON VEGETABLE OIL

5 TO 6 SCALLIONS, WHITES MINCED, GREENS CUT INTO 2-INCH PIECES

1 TABLESPOON FRESH GINGER, PEELED AND MINCED

1 TABLESPOON FRESH GARLIC, PEELED AND MINCED

¼ POUND BUTTON MUSHROOMS

½ WHITE ONION, SLICED

½ CUP BEAN SPROUTS

1 CARROT, CUT INTO MATCHSTICKS

2 POUNDS LO MEIN NOODLES

In a large mixing bowl, add the sesame oil, soy sauce, black vinegar, brown sugar, and fish sauce and whisk to combine. Set aside until the noodles have been cooked.

Place the vegetable oil, scallion whites, ginger, and garlic in a Dutch oven and cook over high heat for 2 minutes. Add the mushrooms, onion, bean sprouts, and carrot and cook for 2 to 3 minutes, until the vegetables are cooked but still crisp. Remove the mixture from the pan and set aside to cool.

Wipe out the pot and bring 3 quarts of water to boil. Add the noodles and cook for 5 to 7 minutes until al dente. Drain and add the noodles to the mixing bowl with the dressing. Toss to coat and add the vegetables and the scallion greens. Serve hot or store in the refrigerator for up to 2 days.

Tips: To keep this dish vegetarian, substitute 2 additional tablespoons of soy sauce for the fish sauce.

If you're in need of protein, add ½ pound of small shrimp to the pan while you are cooking the vegetables.

BAKING/ ROASTING PAN

Your baking cookware isn't just for cookies, cakes, and other confections: it is also great for savory preparations. The crusty exterior and tender inside provided by oven-roasting guarantee a delicious, decadent meal. The dishes in this chapter will work all year long, but their true purpose is keeping you and your loved ones warm and happy once the temperatures start to plummet. They are also perfect for holiday gatherings. If you're looking to make something that will stick in people's minds, consider the Cornish Game Hens with Baby Brussels Sprouts and Caramelized Onions (see page 196). It's a simple yet elegant dish that is sure to impress.

ROAST BEEF AU JUS
WITH VEGETABLES

YIELD: *6 SERVINGS*	ACTIVE TIME: *25 MINUTES*	START TO FINISH: *1 HOUR AND 30 MINUTES*

The bright sweetness provided by the beets makes this dish perfect for those days when winter is beating you down.

- 1 RED BEET, PEELED AND SLICED THIN
- 1 CARROT, MINCED
- 1 PARSNIP, MINCED
- 2 CELERY STALKS, DICED
- 1 YELLOW ONION, PEELED AND CUT INTO ½-INCH THICK SLICES
- 1 ANAHEIM PEPPER, SEEDED AND DICED
- 3 GARLIC CLOVES, MINCED
- 1 TABLESPOON DRIED SAGE
- 1 TABLESPOON GRANULATED GARLIC
- 1 CUP BEEF STOCK
- 1 CUP DRY RED WINE
- 2 TABLESPOONS WORCESTERSHIRE SAUCE
- 2 TABLESPOONS EXTRA VIRGIN OLIVE OIL
- 4 TABLESPOONS FRESH THYME, MINCED
- 1 (2-POUND) EYE OF ROUND BEEF ROAST
- SALT AND PEPPER TO TASTE

Preheat oven to 375°F. Place all of the ingredients, besides the olive oil, 2 tablespoons of the thyme, and the roast, in a 9 x 13-inch baking pan. Season with salt and pepper and stir to evenly coat the vegetables.

Liberally coat the roast on all sides with the olive oil. Season with salt, pepper, and the remaining thyme and place in the baking pan. Place the pan in the oven and cook until the interior of the roast reads 120°F on a digital thermometer, about 40 to 45 minutes. Remove the pan from the oven and place the roast upside down on a cutting board. Cover with foil and let rest for 15 to 20 minutes before carving.

Use a slotted spoon to transfer the vegetables to a serving dish. Ladle the juices in the pan into a separate bowl.

Cutting against the grain, carve the meat into 1- to 2-inch thick slices. Divide the vegetables between the plates and top with 2 or 3 slices of roast beef. Spoon the juices over the top and serve.

NO-BOIL BAKED MANICOTTI

YIELD: *4 TO 6 SERVINGS*	ACTIVE TIME: *15 MINUTES*	START TO FINISH: *1 HOUR AND 15 MINUTES*

The blend of veal and beef adds a little complexity to this manicotti amidst all that rich, melted cheese.

2 TABLESPOONS EXTRA VIRGIN OLIVE OIL

1 LARGE WHITE ONION, DICED

3 TO 4 GARLIC CLOVES, MINCED

SALT AND PEPPER TO TASTE

1 POUND GROUND BEEF (85% LEAN)

1 POUND GROUND VEAL

1 TABLESPOON DRIED OREGANO

½ TABLESPOON GRANULATED GARLIC

½ TABLESPOON GRANULATED ONION

PINCH OF CRUSHED RED PEPPER FLAKES

2 CUPS RICOTTA MIXTURE (SEE PAGE 213)

2 TABLESPOONS FRESH BASIL, CHOPPED

15 TO 18 MANICOTTI SHELLS

4 CUPS SLOW MARINARA (SEE PAGE 87)

1 CUP PARMESAN CHEESE, GRATED

1 CUP MOZZARELLA, GRATED

2 TABLESPOONS FRESH PARSLEY, CHOPPED, FOR GARNISH

Preheat oven to 400°F. Place the olive oil in a sauté pan and warm over medium-high heat. Add the onion and garlic and cook for 5 to 7 minutes, or until the onions are translucent. Season with salt and pepper and add the beef, veal, oregano, granulated garlic, granulated onion, and crushed red pepper flakes. Cook for about 10 minutes, using a wooden spoon to break the meat apart. When the meat is browned, drain the fat from the pot and let the mixture cool for 10 minutes.

Combine the contents of the sauté pan with the ricotta mixture. Fold in the basil, then divide the mixture between the manicotti shells. Place the stuffed shells in a 9 x 13-inch baking pan, top with the Slow Marinara, and cover the pan with foil.

Place in the oven and bake for 35 to 40 minutes, or until the noodles are fully cooked and the filling is hot.

Remove the foil, top with the Parmesan and mozzarella, and return to oven until the cheese is melted. Garnish with parsley and serve.

Tip: This recipe freezes very well. If you want to get it ready ahead of time, perform Steps 1 and 2 and then wrap the pan in plastic wrap. Store in the freezer and transfer to the refrigerator to thaw 1 day before you want to serve it.

PESTO LEG OF LAMB WITH LEMON LENTILS AND ROASTED TOMATOES

YIELD: *4 TO 6 SERVINGS*	ACTIVE TIME: *15 MINUTES*	START TO FINISH: *2 DAYS*

Yes, you'll have to wait awhile, but it's worth it. Giving the pesto and the lamb 2 days together before searing and roasting makes all the difference in this dish.

PESTO

¼ POUND FRESH BASIL LEAVES

⅓ CUP RAW WALNUTS, SHELLED

1 TO 2 GARLIC CLOVES, PEELED

ZEST AND JUICE OF ½ A LEMON

SALT AND PEPPER TO TASTE

½ CUP EXTRA VIRGIN OLIVE OIL

½ CUP PARMESAN CHEESE,
  SHREDDED OR GRATED

**LEG OF LAMB WITH
LEMON LENTILS AND
ROASTED TOMATOES**

2 POUNDS BONELESS LEG OF
  LAMB

2 CUPS GREEN OR BROWN
  LENTILS, RINSED

4 CUPS BEEF OR LAMB STOCK

1 CARROT, WASHED AND
  MINCED

1 YELLOW ONION, PEELED AND
  MINCED

6 TO 12 TOMATOES "ON THE
  VINE," LEFT WHOLE OR
  DICED

ZEST AND JUICE OF ½ A LEMON

SALT AND PEPPER TO TASTE

PESTO

Place the basil leaves, walnuts, garlic, lemon zest, and lemon juice in a food processor or a blender. Season with salt and pepper and puree for 30 seconds to 1 minute. Add the olive oil and puree until smooth. Add the Parmesan cheese and pulse until incorporated. Make sure not to puree for too long or the mixture could get hot, causing the cheese to clump. Season with salt and pepper and transfer 1 cup of the pesto to a plastic bag.

Place the leg of lamb in the bag containing the pesto and refrigerate for 2 days. Store the rest of the pesto in an airtight container.

LEG OF LAMB WITH LEMON LENTILS AND ROASTED TOMATOES

When the lamb has finished marinating, preheat the oven to 400°F. Place the lentils, stock, carrot, onion, and, if you elect to dice them, the tomatoes in a 9 x 13-inch baking pan.

This step is optional, but recommended. Place a cast-iron skillet over medium-high heat and add the leg of lamb. Sear until a dark brown crust forms, turn over, and sear the other side. Remove the lamb from the skillet and place on top of the lentils.

Cover the dish with foil and place in the oven for 1 hour, or until the lentils are soft but not mushy.

If you choose to leave the tomatoes whole, place them in the skillet and sprinkle with olive oil and salt. When the lamb has 10 minutes left to cook, place the skillet in the oven.

Remove the baking pan and, if roasting the tomatoes, the skillet from the oven. Uncover the baking pan and transfer the lamb to a cutting board. Let rest for 10 minutes before carving. Stir the lemon zest and lemon juice into the lentils.

When carving the lamb, make sure you cut against the grain. Stir the remaining pesto into the lentils or serve it on the side with the roasted tomatoes.

PORK ROULADE WITH ORANGES, RAINBOW CHARD, AND WILD RICE

YIELD: *6 SERVINGS*	**ACTIVE TIME:** *30 TO 45 MINUTES*	**START TO FINISH:** *60 TO 90 MINUTES*

Roulades are a great way to pack flavor into a single piece of meat, as this floral, citrus-packed meal shows.

1 (3 TO 4 POUND) PORK LOIN, BUTTERFLIED ½-INCH THICK AND ROLLED OUT FLAT

SALT AND PEPPER TO TASTE

1 TEASPOON GROUND FENNEL SEEDS

1 TEASPOON GROUND CELERY SEEDS

2 ORANGES, ZESTED AND THEN SLICED INTO ¼-INCH THICK ROUNDS

8 STALKS OF RAINBOW CHARD, STEMS REMOVED AND MINCED, LEAVES RESERVED

2 TABLESPOONS OLIVE OIL

2 GARLIC CLOVES, MINCED

1 FENNEL BULB, SLICED VERY THIN

1 CUP WILD RICE

2½ CUPS CHICKEN STOCK

2 PLUM TOMATOES, MINCED

Preheat oven to 350°F. Season both sides of the butterflied pork loin with salt and pepper. Sprinkle the fennel seeds, celery seeds, and orange zest across the interior of the pork loin. Lay the leaves of chard across the interior and then roll the pork loin up until it is closed.

Cut a 3-foot section of kitchen twine and use it to tie the rolled-up pork loin closed. Drizzle the olive oil over the pork and rub it in. Place the pork roulade in a cast-iron skillet and cook over medium-high heat for 3 to 5 minutes on each side.

Place the remaining ingredients in a 9 x 13-inch baking pan. Place the seared pork loin in the center of the pan and top with the orange slices. Wrap the pan tightly with foil and cook for 45 minutes to 1 hour, until the center of the pork reaches 145°F and the rice is tender.

Remove the pan from the oven and place the pork loin on a cutting board. Cover it with foil and let rest for 15 minutes before removing the twine and carving. If the rice is not tender, cover the pan with foil and return to the oven until it is ready.

Tip: To butterfly the pork loin, you'll want to use a sharp knife and cut the pork loin lengthwise, taking care not to cut all the way through. Roll it out and repeat until the pork loin can lie flat and is ½ to 1 inch thick. If you don't think your knife skills are up to the task, you can always ask a butcher to do it for you.

MAPLE MUSTARD PORK LOIN WITH POTATOES AND ONIONS

YIELD: *6 SERVINGS*	**ACTIVE TIME:** *15 TO 20 MINUTES*	**START TO FINISH:** *1 HOUR AND 30 MINUTES*

I find that oven-roasted meats help keep the blues away when the cold weather comes. The sweetness of the maple syrup in this dish doesn't hurt either.

2 POUNDS RED POTATOES, CUT
INTO WEDGES

2 YELLOW ONIONS, CUT INTO
½-INCH THICK SLICES

4 CELERY STALKS, CUT INTO
5-INCH PIECES

½ POUND CARROTS, WASHED AND
SPLIT LENGTHWISE

3 TABLESPOONS EXTRA VIRGIN
OLIVE OIL

SALT AND PEPPER TO TASTE

2½ POUNDS PORK LOIN

¼ CUP REAL MAPLE SYRUP

5 GARLIC CLOVES, MINCED

1 CUP CHICKEN OR VEGETABLE
STOCK

3 BAY LEAVES

Preheat oven to 375°F degrees. In a 9 x 13-inch baking pan, place the potatoes, onions, celery, and carrots. Add 2 tablespoons of the extra virgin olive oil, season with salt and pepper, and toss to coat. Cover the pan with foil and bake in the oven for 30 minutes.

While the vegetables are cooking, rub the pork loin with the maple syrup and the remaining olive oil. Season with salt and pepper and let the pork come to room temperature.

Remove the pan from the oven, remove the foil, and set aside. Add the garlic, stock, and bay leaves. Place the pork loin on top of the vegetables and return the pan to the oven. Cook for 45 to 50 minutes, or until the center of the pork reaches 145°F. Cooking times will vary in different ovens, so make sure you check the pork after it has been cooking for 30 minutes.

Remove the pan from the oven and transfer the pork loin to a cutting board. Place the reserved foil over it and let the pork rest for 10 to 15 minutes.

Remove the carrots, celery, 1 cup of the onions, and the juices from the pan. Transfer to a blender and puree until smooth. Remember to vent the blender slightly so that the steam can escape.

Slice the pork loin into 1-inch thick pieces. Place the potatoes and onions on the serving plates and top with the pork and sauce.

Tips: If possible, avoid using artificial maple syrup in this dish.

It is not necessary to use the blender for the sauce. Simply spooning the juices over the pork will provide a thinner, but still flavorful, sauce.

BAKED CHICKEN CORDON BLEU

YIELD: *6 SERVINGS*	**ACTIVE TIME:** *25 MINUTES*	**START TO FINISH:** *1 HOUR AND 15 MINUTES*

*Here's a lighter version of this classic breaded chicken dish.
Don't worry—between the ham, cheese, and buttery vegetables,
there's more than enough flavor remaining.*

2 ZUCCHINI, CUT INTO 1-INCH
THICK SLICES ON A BIAS

2 SUMMER SQUASH, CUT INTO
1-INCH THICK SLICES ON A
BIAS

2 LARGE LEEKS, WHITE PARTS
ONLY, WASHED AND CUT
INTO 1-INCH PIECES

¼ CUP EXTRA VIRGIN OLIVE OIL,
PLUS 2 TABLESPOONS

2 TABLESPOONS DRIED OREGANO

SALT AND PEPPER TO TASTE

6 (5 OZ.) BONELESS, SKINLESS
CHICKEN BREASTS

12 SLICES OF HAM (I LIKE TO
USE EITHER HONEY HAM OR
VIRGINIA HAM)

12 SLICES OF SWISS CHEESE

1½ CUPS SEASONED BREAD
CRUMBS

2 TABLESPOONS FRESH CHIVES,
MINCED, FOR GARNISH

2 TABLESPOONS FRESH BASIL,
MINCED, FOR GARNISH

Preheat the oven to 375°F. In a 9 x 13-inch baking dish, add the vegetables, ¼ cup of the olive oil, and the dried oregano. Season with salt and pepper and toss to coat evenly.

Place the chicken breasts on a cutting board and cut horizontally through the middle, stopping about 1 inch short of the opposite edge to keep the breasts in one piece.

Lay each piece of chicken open, cover with a piece of plastic wrap or parchment paper, and use a kitchen mallet to pound the breasts until each one is about ¼ inch thick. You want to hit the breasts lightly in the center, working toward the outside edge. If you don't have a mallet, a small sauté pan or rolling pin will also work.

Season the inside of chicken breasts with salt and pepper. Place 2 pieces of ham on top of each breast. Place 2 pieces of Swiss cheese on top of the ham. Fold the chicken breasts so that they resemble their original shapes.

Nestle the chicken breasts into the vegetables in the baking pan. Rub each breast with the remaining olive oil and sprinkle the bread crumbs on top.

Cover the pan tightly with foil and place it in the oven. Bake until the centers of the chicken breasts read 165°F on a digital thermometer. Remove the chicken from the pan and let rest for 5 minutes before slicing. Garnish with the chives and basil and serve.

Tip: Making your own seasoned bread crumbs is easy and worth the effort, since you can control the amount of seasoning. Take half of a French baguette (or any crusty or slightly stale bread), add it to a food processor, and process until broken down into fine crumbs. Add 2 tablespoons of extra virgin olive oil and 1 tablespoon each of dried oregano, dried basil, salt, and pepper. Pulse until combined.

CHIPOTLE CHICKEN ENCHILADAS

YIELD: *4 TO 6 SERVINGS*	**ACTIVE TIME:** *25 MINUTES*	**START TO FINISH:** *1 HOUR AND 30 MINUTES*

I love making enchiladas because you can tailor them to your whims. This version utilizes a smoky, slightly spicy dried chipotle sauce.

ENCHILADA SAUCE

4 DRIED CHIPOTLE CHILIES

½ (7 OZ.) CAN DICED MILD GREEN CHILIES

2 TABLESPOONS CANOLA OIL (OR PREFERRED NEUTRAL OIL)

2 TO 3 PLUM TOMATOES, SEEDED

1 TABLESPOON TOMATO PASTE

1 TABLESPOON CUMIN

1 TEASPOON DRIED OREGANO

SALT AND PEPPER TO TASTE

FILLING

4 TABLESPOONS CANOLA OIL (OR PREFERRED NEUTRAL OIL)

4 TO 6 BONELESS, SKINLESS CHICKEN THIGHS

SALT AND PEPPER TO TASTE

2 CUPS CHICKEN STOCK

1 TO 2 RUSSET POTATOES, PEELED AND MINCED

½ CUP WHITE ONION, MINCED

2 GARLIC CLOVES, MINCED

½ (7 OZ.) CAN DICED MILD GREEN CHILIES

1 TABLESPOON ENCHILADA SAUCE

16 TO 24 CORN TORTILLAS

1 CUP COTIJA CHEESE, CRUMBLED, FOR GARNISH

CILANTRO, CHOPPED, FOR GARNISH

ENCHILADA SAUCE

Bring 2 cups of water to boil in a large cast-iron skillet. Add the chipotle chilies and cook until soft, about 10 minutes. Drain and transfer the chilies to a blender or food processor. Add the remaining ingredients and puree until smooth. Add the puree to the skillet and cook over medium-low heat until thick enough to coat the back of a spoon, about 15 to 20 minutes. Remove the sauce from the pan and set aside. Wipe out the skillet.

FILLING

Place the cast-iron skillet over medium-high heat and warm 2 tablespoons of the oil. Season the chicken with salt and pepper and add the chicken to the pan. Sear on both sides, then add 1½ cups of the chicken stock. Cover and cook until you can shred the chicken with a fork, about 15 to 20 minutes. Remove the chicken, transfer to a bowl, and shred with two forks.

Add the remaining oil and the potatoes to the skillet. Cook for 5 minutes while stirring. Add the onion and garlic and cook for 5 minutes, or until the onions start to caramelize. Stir often to avoid burning the vegetables.

Continued...

Tip: If you cannot find dried chipotles, you can use canned chipotle peppers in adobo sauce. Be aware that they are spicier. A 7 oz. can will be enough for this preparation, and there is no need to boil them before adding to the blender.

Reduce the heat to medium. Add the shredded chicken, the remaining stock, the green chilies, and the Enchilada Sauce. Cook until the chicken stock has evaporated, about 5 to 10 minutes. Remove the filling from the pan and set aside. Wipe the pan clean and place over medium-low heat.

Preheat the oven to 375°F and grease a 9 x 13-inch baking pan with cooking spray. Working with one tortilla at a time, place the tortillas in the skillet and cook on each side for 20 seconds. Transfer the heated tortillas to a work surface and spread a small amount of sauce on each of them. Evenly distribute the filling between the tortillas and roll them up. Place the tortillas seam side down in the baking dish.

Top the enchiladas with the remaining sauce and place in the oven. Bake for 20 minutes, or until a crust forms on the exterior of the tortillas. Garnish with the Cotija cheese and cilantro and serve.

BAKED TOMATILLO CHICKEN CASSEROLE

YIELD: *6 SERVINGS*	**ACTIVE TIME:** *15 MINUTES*	**START TO FINISH:** *24 HOURS*

Packed with shredded chicken and tangy tomatillos,
this casserole showcases the flavors of the Southwest.

MARINADE

1 TOMATILLO, HUSK REMOVED, RINSED AND HALVED

1 PLUM TOMATO, HALVED

2 GARLIC CLOVES

1 SHALLOT, PEELED AND HALVED

1 POBLANO PEPPER, HALVED AND SEEDED

¼ CUP CANOLA OIL (OR PREFERRED NEUTRAL OIL)

1 TABLESPOON KOSHER SALT

1 TABLESPOON CUMIN

SALSA VERDE

6 TOMATILLOS, HUSKS REMOVED, RINSED

8 TO 10 SERRANO PEPPERS, RINSED AND STEMMED

½ WHITE ONION

2 GARLIC CLOVES, MINCED

KOSHER SALT TO TASTE

¼ CUP OIL

CILANTRO, CHOPPED

Continued...

MARINADE

Place all of the ingredients in a blender and blend until smooth. Pour over the chicken breasts and refrigerate overnight.

SALSA VERDE

Place the tomatillos and serrano peppers in a large saucepan and cover with water. Bring to a boil and cook until the tomatillos start to lose their bright green color, about 10 minutes. Drain the water and transfer to a blender. Add the remaining ingredients and puree until smooth. Top with the cilantro and set aside.

Continued...

CHICKEN CASSEROLE

2½ POUNDS BONELESS, SKINLESS
    CHICKEN BREASTS, SLICED
    THIN

2 EGGS, BEATEN

1 (14 OZ.) CAN OF FIRE-ROASTED
    TOMATOES

PINCH OF SALT

14 CORN TORTILLAS

1 CUP SALSA VERDE

¼ CUP COTIJA OR FETA CHEESE,
    CRUMBLED

CHICKEN CASSEROLE

Preheat the oven to 375°F. Place the chicken and marinade in an 8 x 8-inch baking pan, place it in the oven, and cook until the center of the chicken reaches 165°F. Remove the pan from the oven, remove the chicken, and leave the marinade in the pan. Transfer the chicken to a mixing bowl and shred with a fork. Add the eggs, fire-roasted tomatoes, and salt and stir to combine.

Place 4 tortillas in the baking dish. Add ½ of the chicken mixture, top with four tortillas, and add the remaining chicken mixture. Top with remaining tortillas, cover with the salsa verde, and then place in the oven. Bake for about 30 minutes until the center is hot. Remove, sprinkle the cheese on top, and return to the oven until it is melted. Remove, cut into 6 pieces, and serve.

Tips: You can use a store-bought version of salsa verde, but the homemade version provided here is way better. If you cannot find serrano peppers, use jalapeños and cut the amount in half. If you don't want the salsa to be too spicy, omit the serranos entirely and replace with 1 poblano pepper.

Cotija is a creamy, salty Mexican cheese. If you can't find it, feta or goat cheese are good replacements.

CORNISH GAME HENS WITH BABY BRUSSELS SPROUTS AND CARAMELIZED ONIONS

YIELD: 4 SERVINGS	ACTIVE TIME: 20 TO 30 MINUTES	TOTAL TIME: 3 TO 9 HOURS

I love making this for dinner parties, since there is something so elegant about everyone getting their own hen.

BRINE (OPTIONAL)

5 CUPS WATER

1 CUP SUGAR

1 CUP SALT

2 BAY LEAVES

1 TABLESPOON BLACK
    PEPPERCORNS, GROUND

1 TABLESPOON CORIANDER SEEDS,
    GROUND

½ TABLESPOON FENNEL SEEDS,
    GROUND

½ TABLESPOON CELERY SEEDS,
    GROUND

Continued...

BRINE

In a large stockpot, add the water, sugar, and salt and cook over medium-high heat until the sugar and salt dissolve. Add the remaining ingredients, remove from heat, and let cool to room temperature. Place the Cornish game hens in the brine, making sure they are completely covered, using a small bowl to weigh them down. Soak in the brine for 4 to 6 hours.

CORNISH GAME HENS WITH BABY BRUSSELS SPROUTS AND CARMELIZED ONIONS

Preheat the oven to 375°F.

Place the thyme, sage, rosemary, and minced garlic in a bowl and stir until combined.

Remove the Cornish game hens from the brine, pat dry, and rub with olive oil. Sprinkle with salt, pepper, and the herb-and-garlic mixture. Let the game hens stand at room temperature for approximately 30 minutes.

In a Dutch oven, add 3 tablespoons of olive oil, the smashed garlic cloves, onion, and 1 tablespoon of salt. Cook over medium-high heat, reducing the heat if the onion starts to burn or dry out, until the onion is dark brown. Remove from the pan and set aside.

Place the Brussels sprouts, the remaining olive oil, and the pinch of salt in the Dutch oven. Stir until the brussels sprouts are evenly coated.

Continued...

CORNISH GAME HENS WITH BABY BRUSSELS SPROUTS AND CARAMELIZED ONIONS

4 (3-POUND) CORNISH GAME
    HENS

1½ TABLESPOONS FRESH THYME,
    MINCED

1½ TABLESPOONS SAGE, MINCED

1½ TABLESPOONS ROSEMARY,
    MINCED

11 GARLIC CLOVES, 3 MINCED, 8
    SMASHED

5 TABLESPOONS EXTRA VIRGIN
    OLIVE OIL, PLUS MORE FOR
    RUBBING

1 LARGE WHITE ONION, SLICED

1 TABLESPOON KOSHER SALT,
    PLUS 1 PINCH

2 POUNDS BABY BRUSSELS
    SPROUTS (IF YOU CAN'T FIND
    BABY BRUSSELS SPROUTS,
    CUT REGULAR-SIZED
    BRUSSELS SPROUTS IN HALF)

1 LEMON, QUARTERED; PLUS ½ OF
    A LEMON

¼ CUP BUTTER

Spread brussels sprouts into a layer in a 9 x 13-inch baking pan, cover with a layer of the garlic-and-onion mixture, and place the Cornish hens in the pan, breast side up. Put the ½ of a lemon in the center of the pan. Place the lemon quarters against the edge of the pan and between each hen. Place the pan in the oven and cook for 30 to 40 minutes.

Raise the heat to 400°F, remove the pan from the oven, and spin each hen 180°. Rub the top of each with the butter, return the pan to the oven, and cook for 20 minutes, or until the internal temperature of each hen is 165°F. Remove pan from the oven and let stand for up to 30 minutes before serving.

Tips: Brining will help the hens retain moisture, and keep them from getting dry if you overcook them.

If you plan on removing and discarding the skin after the hens are cooked, try cooking them breast side down, as this will ensure that they are even juicier.

JAMAICAN JERK CHICKEN WITH ROOT VEGETABLES

YIELD: *6 SERVINGS*	**ACTIVE TIME:** *15 MINUTES*	**START TO FINISH:** *24 HOURS*

I fell in love with the flavors I encountered while visiting Jamaica, and rushed to my kitchen to try and recreate them when I got home. The root vegetables are a nice twist on the rice and beans that are traditionally served with jerk chicken.

JAMAICAN JERK CHICKEN WITH ROOT VEGETABLES

MARINADE (SEE PAGE 201)

5 POUNDS BONE-IN CHICKEN PIECES

1 CUP RED BEETS, PEELED AND DICED

1 CUP CARROTS, PEELED AND DICED

1½ CUPS SWEET POTATOES, PEELED AND DICED

1 CUP TURNIPS, PEELED AND DICED

1 YUCCA ROOT, PEELED AND DICED

¼ CUP VEGETABLE OIL

SALT AND PEPPER, TO TASTE

2 TABLESPOONS FRESH THYME

Continued...

JAMAICAN JERK CHICKEN WITH ROOT VEGETABLES

Pour the marinade into a mixing bowl, add the chicken pieces, cover, and refrigerate overnight.

Preheat the oven to 375°F.

Place the vegetables, oil, salt, and pepper in an 11 x 15-inch baking pan and roast for 30 minutes. Remove, add the thyme, return the pan to the oven, and cook for 25 more minutes.

Remove the pan from the oven. Shake any excess marinade from the chicken and place it on top of the vegetables. Return the pan to the oven and cook for 45 to 50 minutes, until the thickest parts of the chicken reach 165°F. Remove the pan from the oven and serve.

MARINADE

2 TABLESPOONS FRESH THYME

3 HABANERO PEPPERS, SEEDS
    REMOVED FROM 2

½ YELLOW ONION

½ CUP BROWN SUGAR

½ TABLESPOON CINNAMON

½ TEASPOON NUTMEG

1 TABLESPOON ALLSPICE

2 TABLESPOONS FRESH GINGER,
    PEELED

1 CUP CANOLA OIL (OR PREFERRED
    NEUTRAL OIL)

2 TABLESPOONS SOY SAUCE

1 SCALLION

1 TABLESPOON SALT

1 TABLESPOON PEPPER

1 TABLESPOON RICE VINEGAR

MARINADE

Place all of the ingredients in a blender and puree until smooth.

Tip: Try using a spoon to peel the ginger for the marinade. This is a trick I learned while working in restaurants and it will save you plenty of time and frustration.

CITRUS AND SAGE CHICKEN WITH GOLDEN BEETS

YIELD: *6 SERVINGS*	ACTIVE TIME: *30 MINUTES*	START TO FINISH: *3 HOURS AND 40 MINUTES*

*This dish was made for the dead of winter,
when citrus and root vegetables reach their sweetest point.*

MARINADE

3 GARLIC CLOVES

⅓ CUP SAGE LEAVES

ZEST AND JUICE OF 1 ORANGE

1 TABLESPOON CORIANDER

½ TABLESPOON BLACK PEPPER

½ TEASPOON CRUSHED RED PEPPER FLAKES

¼ CUP EXTRA VIRGIN OLIVE OIL

1 TABLESPOON KOSHER SALT

1 TABLESPOON SHALLOT, MINCED

CITRUS AND SAGE CHICKEN WITH GOLDEN BEETS

3 POUNDS BONE-IN, SKIN-ON CHICKEN
    THIGHS

2 POUNDS GOLDEN BEETS, PEELED AND CUT
    INTO WEDGES

2 TABLESPOONS EXTRA VIRGIN OLIVE OIL

SALT AND PEPPER TO TASTE

1 CUP GRAPEFRUIT JUICE

4 LEEKS, WHITES ONLY, WASHED AND
    SLICED INTO ¼-INCH THICK HALF-
    MOONS

1½ SHALLOTS, MINCED

4 TABLESPOONS BUTTER,
    CUT INTO 6 PIECES

MARINADE

Add all of the ingredients to a blender and blend until smooth. If not using a blender, mince all of the ingredients and whisk together in a bowl.

CITRUS AND SAGE CHICKEN WITH GOLDEN BEETS

Pour the marinade over the chicken thighs and marinate for 2 hours. Preheat the oven to 375°F. Place the beets in a roasting pan and toss with the oil, salt, and pepper. Pour in the grapefruit juice, place the pan in the oven, and roast for 50 minutes.

Remove pan from oven, drain the grapefruit juice, and reserve. Raise temperature to 400°F. Add the leeks and shallots to the pan and stir to combine. Push the vegetables to the outside of pan and nestle the chicken thighs, skin-side up, in the center. Place in the oven and cook for 40 minutes.

Remove the pan from the oven and pour the grapefruit juice over the chicken. Turn the oven to the broiler setting. Place one piece of butter on each piece of chicken, place the pan under the broiler, and cook for 10 minutes, until the chicken is 165°F in the center. The beets should still have a slight snap to them and the skin of the chicken should be crispy.

SPATCHCOCKED LEMON AND THYME CHICKEN WITH VEGETABLES

| **YIELD:** *4 TO 6 SERVINGS* | **ACTIVE TIME:** *30 MINUTES* | **START TO FINISH:** *2 HOURS AND 30 MINUTES* |

If you are looking to cut your cooking time in half and get that crispy skin that always seems so evasive, this recipe will help you accomplish both. Salting the chicken and letting it rest before cooking will draw moisture to the top and keep your chicken from getting dry in the oven.

1 2- TO 3-POUND WHOLE CHICKEN, SPATCHCOCKED

2 TABLESPOONS KOSHER SALT, PLUS MORE TO TASTE

1 LEMON, CUT INTO 1 (½-INCH THICK) WHEEL; REMAINDER SLICED VERY THIN

1 TABLESPOON DIJON MUSTARD

4 TABLESPOONS FRESH THYME, MINCED

BLACK PEPPER TO TASTE

1 VIDALIA ONION, CUT INTO THICK SLICES

1 TURNIP, PEELED AND CHOPPED

2 CARROTS, CHOPPED

2 PARSNIPS, CHOPPED

2 CUPS CELERY, CHOPPED

2 RUSSET POTATOES, SCRUBBED AND CHOPPED

¼ CUP EXTRA VIRGIN OLIVE OIL

Rinse the chicken under cold running water and pat dry with a paper towel. Sprinkle the 2 tablespoons kosher salt over the chicken and let sit for 30 minutes.

Preheat the oven to 400°F. Rinse the chicken and pat dry. Make slits where the legs and breast meet to expose the meat under the skin. Cut the ½-inch thick lemon wheel in half and place one piece into each slit. Fold the legs back over and rub the mustard over the chicken. Sprinkle with additional salt, 2 tablespoons of the thyme, and the pepper. Let chicken sit for 30 minutes.

Place the vegetables and the olive oil in a basking/roasting pan. Add the remaining thyme and season with salt and pepper. Stir to coat the vegetables, place the pan in the oven, and cook for 30 minutes.

Remove the pan from the oven and stir the vegetables. If using a baking pan, place an oven-safe rack on top of the vegetables. Place the chicken on the rack. This will keep the vegetables underneath the chicken from getting overly soggy. Place the remaining slices of lemon on top of the chicken in an even layer. Return the pan to the for 40 minutes to 1 hour, until the interior of the chicken breast is 160°F to 165°F.

Remove the pan from the oven and set the chicken aside. Cover with foil and let stand for 15 minutes before carving. If the vegetables are still a bit firm, stir and return pan to the oven until they are more to your liking.

Tip: Spatchcocking is removing a chicken's backbone and laying the chicken flat to ensure that it cooks evenly and that the skin gets crispy. To spatchcock a chicken, place it breast down on a work surface. Take kitchen shears or a knife and cut along the backbone on both sides from top to bottom. Flip the chicken over so that it is breast side up. It should lay flat. Discard the backbone or reserve it for stock.

ROSEMARY BALSAMIC CHICKEN WITH WILD RICE

YIELD: *4 TO 6 SERVINGS*	**ACTIVE TIME:** *15 TO 20 MINUTES*	**START TO FINISH:** *2 HOURS AND 30 MINUTES*

Chicken braised until it is falling off the bone is just the beginning for this dish—the robust flavor of the brussels sprouts and the tanginess of the balsamic vinegar push it over the top.

2 TABLESPOONS KOSHER SALT, PLUS MORE TO TASTE

4 TABLESPOONS EXTRA VIRGIN OLIVE OIL

4 TABLESPOONS BALSAMIC VINEGAR

3 TABLESPOONS FRESH ROSEMARY, PLUS 2 TABLESPOONS, DICED

BLACK PEPPER TO TASTE

5 LARGE OR 10 SMALL CHICKEN DRUMSTICKS

1½ CUPS BRUSSELS SPROUTS, HALVED LENGTHWISE

1 CUP WILD RICE

2⅓ CUPS CHICKEN STOCK

3 GARLIC CLOVES, MINCED

1 PARSNIP, PEELED AND MINCED

½ YELLOW ONION, PEELED AND MINCED

Preheat the oven to 400°F. Place the salt, olive oil, balsamic vinegar, and 3 tablespoons of rosemary in a bowl. Season with pepper, stir to combine, and add the chicken. Stir until the chicken is coated and then place the contents of the bowl in a roasting pan. Place the pan in the oven and cook for 30 minutes.

Toss the Brussels sprouts with the remaining olive oil and balsamic vinegar. Season with salt and pepper and set aside.

When the chicken has cooked for 30 minutes, remove the pan from the oven, turn the chicken over, and add the brussels sprouts. Return the pan to the oven and cook for 20 minutes, until the brussels sprouts start to caramelize.

Remove the pan from the oven, remove the chicken and the brussels sprouts from the pan, and set aside. Place the rice, chicken stock, garlic, parsnip, and onion in the pan. Nestle the drumsticks into the rice so that the bone points toward the center. Cover the pan and cook for 50 minutes to 1 hour, until the rice is fully cooked. Remove the pan from the oven, remove the cover, and return the brussels sprouts to the pan. Briefly return the pan to the oven to warm the Brussels sprouts. Sprinkle with the remaining rosemary and serve.

Tip: If you don't have a roasting pan lid, you can use aluminum foil.

ROASTED CHICKEN AND PASTA BAKE

YIELD: *4 TO 6 SERVINGS*	**ACTIVE TIME:** *30 MINUTES*	**START TO FINISH:** *2 HOURS*

The easy cleanup is the second-best part of this meal. The chicken benefits from the lovely balance struck by the spicy peperoncini and the savory mushrooms.

1½ POUNDS BONE-IN, SKIN-ON CHICKEN BREASTS

¼ CUP RED WINE

1 CUP MUSHROOMS, SLICED

¼ CUP CHICKEN STOCK

8 OZ. PASTA (I USE COOKED LASAGNA SHEETS CUT INTO ½-INCH STRIPS)

1 CUP CAMPARI, PLUM, OR ROMA TOMATOES, DICED

1 CUP BEET GREENS, WASHED AND CHOPPED

8 TO 10 PEPERONCINI, HALVED LENGTHWISE

1 CUP ASIAGO CHEESE, SHREDDED, PLUS MORE FOR TOPPING

1 TABLESPOON DRIED OREGANO

1 TEASPOON GARLIC POWDER

½ TEASPOON CRUSHED RED PEPPER FLAKES

ZEST AND JUICE OF 1 LEMON

SALT AND PEPPER TO TASTE

FRESH BASIL, CHOPPED, FOR GARNISH

Preheat the oven to 375°F. Place the chicken breasts, red wine, mushrooms, and chicken stock in a 9 x 13-inch baking pan and bake for 45 to 55 minutes, until the internal temperature of the chicken is 160°F.

While the chicken is cooking, bring water to boil in a medium saucepan and add the pasta. Cook until al dente, drain, and set aside.

Remove the chicken from the oven and let rest for 10 minutes. Remove the skin and bones and discard. Tear the chicken meat into large pieces and return to the pan.

Place the pasta, tomatoes, beet greens, peperoncini, Asiago, oregano, garlic powder, crushed red pepper flakes, lemon juice, lemon zest, salt, and pepper in the baking pan. Top with additional Asiago, place the pan in the oven, and bake for 30 to 40 minutes, or until the mixture in the pan is bubbling.

Remove the pan from the oven, garnish with fresh basil, and serve.

COD WITH SUN-DRIED TOMATO BREAD CRUMBS, ROASTED ASPARAGUS, AND MASHED POTATOES

YIELD: *4 TO 6 SERVINGS*	ACTIVE TIME: *30 TO 45 MINUTES*	START TO FINISH: *60 TO 90 MINUTES*

*Baked cod topped with bread crumbs is as New England as it gets.
I've added sun-dried tomatoes for a little sweetness.*

2 TABLESPOONS SUN-DRIED TOMATOES, MINCED

1 GARLIC CLOVE, MINCED

1 TABLESPOON PARSLEY, MINCED, PLUS MORE FOR GARNISH

1 CUP BREAD CRUMBS

10 TABLESPOONS BUTTER, MELTED

2 POUNDS COD FILLETS, CUT INTO 4 TO 5 OZ. PORTIONS

2 BUNCHES OF ASPARAGUS, BOTTOM 2 INCHES OF THE STEMS REMOVED

2 POUNDS RED CREAMER POTATOES, DICED

EXTRA VIRGIN OLIVE OIL TO TASTE

SALT AND PEPPER TO TASTE

¼ CUP HEAVY CREAM

LEMON SLICES, FOR GARNISH

Preheat the oven to 350°F. Place the sun-dried tomatoes, garlic, parsley, bread crumbs, and 4 tablespoons of the butter in a mixing bowl and stir until the bread crumbs are coated with the butter. Set aside.

Spray a 9 x 13-inch baking pan with cooking spray and then place the pieces of cod on one side. Place the asparagus in the middle and place the potatoes on the other side. Season the potatoes and asparagus with the olive oil, salt, and pepper.

Evenly distribute the bread crumbs over each piece of cod. Place the baking pan in the oven and bake for 10 to 15 minutes, until the fish is cooked through and the potatoes are tender. If the potatoes require more cooking time, remove the cod and the asparagus from the pan and then return it to the oven. Wipe out the bowl and set it aside.

Place the cream, the remaining butter, and the cooked potatoes in the mixing bowl. Season with salt and pepper and then mash with a fork until potatoes are the desired texture.

Place a few pieces of asparagus on a plate and top with a piece of cod. Garnish with additional parsley and the lemon slices. Place a scoop of potatoes on the side of each plate and serve.

Tip: If cod isn't your favorite fish, haddock, pollock, and hake are all good substitutes.

SWEET SAUSAGE STUFFED SHELLS

YIELD: *6 SERVINGS*	**ACTIVE TIME:** *25 MINUTES*	**START TO FINISH:** *1 HOUR*

Another favorite meal from my youth, one we didn't have very often. I've got the sneaking suspicion that those rare appearances were due to the frightening amount of shells I piled on my plate each time.

1½ POUNDS RICOTTA

2 EGGS

1½ CUPS ITALIAN CHEESE BLEND
(EQUAL PARTS ASIAGO,
FONTINA, MOZZARELLA,
PROVOLONE, PARMESAN, AND
ROMANO), PLUS MORE FOR
TOPPING

1 TABLESPOON FRESH MINT,
CHOPPED

½ TABLESPOON SEASONING
BLEND (EQUAL PARTS SALT,
PEPPER, ONION POWDER,
AND GARLIC POWDER)

PINCH OF FRESH GRATED NUTMEG

½ TABLESPOON DRIED BASIL

½ TABLESPOON DRIED OREGANO

½ CUP FRESH PARSLEY, CHOPPED

1 TEASPOON FENNEL SEEDS

4 CUPS SLOW MARINARA
(SEE PAGE 87)

1¼ POUNDS GROUND SWEET
ITALIAN SAUSAGE, CHOPPED

1 BOX JUMBO SHELLS, COOKED IN
SALTED WATER

LEAVES FROM 1 BUNCH OF BASIL,
CHOPPED, FOR GARNISH

Preheat the oven to 375°F. In a mixing bowl, add the ricotta, eggs, 1 cup of the Italian cheese blend, the mint, the seasoning blend, nutmeg, dried basil, oregano, parsley, fennel seeds, and ½ cup of the Slow Marinara and stir to combine. Set mixture aside.

Spread the sausage in the bottom of a 9 x 13-inch baking pan, place it in the oven, and bake for 10 to 15 minutes, until the sausage is cooked through. Drain the fat and add the sausage to the ricotta mixture. Wipe out the baking pan and add enough marinara to coat the bottom of the pan.

Stuff each shell with 2 tablespoons of the sausage-and-ricotta mixture and place them on top of the marinara. You should end up with about 18 to 24 stuffed shells.

Cover the shells with the remaining marinara, place the pan in the oven, and cook for 30 minutes, until the center of the shells are hot. Remove the pan from the oven, sprinkle with the remaining cheese, and return to the oven for 5 minutes. When the cheese is melted, remove the pan from the oven, garnish with fresh basil, and serve.

Tip: If you want to make stuffing the shells easier and a lot less messy, place the ricotta mixture in a large freezer bag, cut off a corner, and squeeze the bag to fill each shell.

SEVEN-CHEESE LASAGNA

YIELD: *6 SERVINGS*	**ACTIVE TIME:** *25 MINUTES*	**START TO FINISH:** *1 HOUR AND 30 MINUTES*

Who can resist a nice cheesy piece of lasagna? Add some buttery garlic bread and a simple salad and you have one of my favorite meals to make for a crowd.

1 TABLESPOON SALT

1 BOX OF LASAGNA NOODLES

1½ POUNDS RICOTTA

2 EGGS

1½ CUPS ITALIAN CHEESE BLEND
(EQUAL PARTS ASIAGO,
FONTINA, MOZZARELLA,
PROVOLONE, PARMESAN, AND
ROMANO), PLUS MORE FOR
TOPPING

½ TABLESPOON SEASONING
BLEND (EQUAL PARTS SALT,
PEPPER, ONION POWDER,
GARLIC POWDER)

PINCH OF FRESH NUTMEG,
GRATED

½ TABLESPOON DRIED BASIL

½ TABLESPOON DRIED OREGANO

½ CUP CHOPPED FRESH PARSLEY

2 CUPS SLOW MARINARA
(SEE PAGE 87)

Preheat the oven to 350°F.

If you're using traditional lasagna noodles, bring water to boil in a large saucepan. Add the salt and lasagna noodles and cook until the noodles are al dente, approximately 10 minutes. Drain in a colander and set aside.

While the water is boiling, place the ricotta, eggs, Italian cheese blend, seasoning blend, nutmeg, basil, oregano, parsley, and 1 cup of the Slow Marinara in a mixing bowl. Stir until combined and set aside.

In an 8 x 8-inch baking pan, ladle just enough marinara to coat the bottom of the dish. Place a layer of noodles on top and cover with ⅓ of the marinara-and-cheese mixture. Alternate layers of the noodles and the mixture until the mixture is used up. Place another layer of noodles on top and cover with marinara.

Place the pan in the oven and bake for 45 minutes. Remove from the oven, sprinkle additional cheese on top, and return to oven. Cook for 5 minutes, or until the cheese is melted. Remove from the oven and let stand for 20 minutes. Top with marinara to taste and serve.

Tip: I like to make the marinara-and-cheese filling in advance and let it sit for a few hours so all of the flavors can come together.

EGGPLANT PARMESAN

YIELD: *6 SERVINGS*	**ACTIVE TIME:** *20 MINUTES*	**START TO FINISH:** *3 HOURS AND 30 MINUTES*

This is lighter than the traditional version, which is fried. I find that frying overwhelms the meaty texture and slight bitterness that makes eggplant such a perfect partner for marinara sauce.

3 LARGE EGGPLANTS, PEELED AND
    SLICED INTO ½-INCH COINS

SALT TO TASTE

5 CUPS SLOW MARINARA
    (SEE PAGE 87)

2 TABLESPOONS KOSHER SALT

2 CUPS ITALIAN CHEESE BLEND
    (EQUAL PARTS ASIAGO,
    FONTINA, MOZZARELLA,
    PROVOLONE, PARMESAN, AND
    ROMANO), PLUS MORE FOR
    TOPPING

¼ CUP FRESH BASIL, JULIENNED

Place the eggplant on a baking tray and season generously with salt. Transfer the tray to the refrigerator and chill for 2 hours.

Preheat the oven to 350°F. Remove the tray from the refrigerator and press the eggplant with paper towels to remove as much moisture as possible. Place the eggplant in a single layer in a 9 x 13-inch baking pan. Top with half of the marinara and half of the cheese. Add another layer of eggplant on top and cover with the remainder of the sauce. Place the pan in the oven for 1 hour, remove, and top with additional cheese and the basil. Return the pan to the oven, cook until the cheese is melted, and serve with garlic bread and a side salad.

MARINATED SESAME TOFU WITH ROASTED GREEN BEANS AND SHIITAKE MUSHROOMS

YIELD: *4 SERVINGS*	**ACTIVE TIME:** *5 MINUTES*	**START TO FINISH:** *2 DAYS*

You may be wary of tofu, but this recipe will make you fall in love. Slow roasting is the key here, as it concentrates all that flavor the tofu soaked up while marinating.

MARINADE

3 TABLESPOONS DARK SOY SAUCE

2 TABLESPOONS RICE VINEGAR

1 TABLESPOON SESAME OIL

1 TABLESPOON HONEY

PINCH OF CINNAMON

PINCH OF BLACK PEPPER

SESAME TOFU WITH ROASTED GREEN BEANS AND SHIITAKE MUSHROOMS

1 (14 OZ.) PACKAGE EXTRA FIRM TOFU, DRAINED AND CUT INTO 1-INCH CUBES

1 POUND FRESH GREEN BEANS

¼ POUND SHIITAKE MUSHROOMS, SLICED

2 TABLESPOONS SESAME OIL

1 TABLESPOON SOY SAUCE

2 TABLESPOONS SESAME SEEDS, FOR GARNISH

MARINADE

Place all of the ingredients in a small bowl and stir to combine. Place the marinade and the tofu into a 1-gallon plastic bag and remove as much air as possible. Place in the refrigerator for 2 days, flipping the bag over at the end of Day 1.

SESAME TOFU WITH ROASTED GREEN BEANS AND SHIITAKE MUSHROOMS

Preheat oven to 375°F. Remove the tofu from the bag. Place the green beans, mushrooms, sesame oil, and soy sauce in the bag and shake.

Line a 9 x 13-inch baking pan with parchment paper and place the tofu on it in a single layer. Place the pan in the oven and bake for 35 minutes. Remove the pan, flip the tofu over, and push to the outer edge of the pan. Add the green bean-and-mushroom mixture, return the pan to the oven, and bake for 15 minutes, or until the green beans are cooked to your preference. Remove the pan from the oven, garnish with the sesame seeds, and serve.

ROASTED BARLEY AND CARROTS WITH PASILLA PEPPERS

YIELD: *4 TO 6 SERVINGS*	**ACTIVE TIME:** *10 MINUTES*	**START TO FINISH:** *2 HOURS*

This dish is light, sweet, spicy, and nutty. Considering how affordable all of the ingredients are, that's whole a lot of taste for not very much money.

5 CARROTS, CUT LENGTHWISE INTO 3-INCH PIECES

EXTRA VIRGIN OLIVE OIL TO TASTE

SALT AND PEPPER TO TASTE

6 DRIED PASILLA PEPPERS

2¼ CUPS WATER

1 CUP PEARL BARLEY

1 CUP RED ONION, MINCED

2 TABLESPOONS ADOBO SEASONING

1 TABLESPOON SUGAR

1 TABLESPOON CHILI POWDER

¼ CUP DRIED OREGANO

Preheat the oven to 375°F. Place the carrots in a 9 x 13-inch baking pan, drizzle with the olive oil, and season with salt and pepper. Place the pan in the oven and roast for 45 to 50 minutes, or until the carrots are slightly soft to the touch.

While the carrots are cooking, open the Pasilla peppers and remove the seeds and stems. Place the peppers in a bowl. Add the water to a saucepan and bring to a boil. Pour the boiling water over the peppers and cover the bowl with plastic.

When the carrots are done, remove the baking pan from the oven, add the remaining ingredients, and pour the liquid from the peppers into the pan. Chop the reconstituted peppers, add to the pan, and stir so that the liquid is covering the barley. Cover the pan tightly with aluminum foil and put it back in oven for another 45 minutes, or until the barley becomes tender. Fluff with a fork and serve.

Tip: Adobo is a spice blend consisting of garlic powder, salt, onion powder, oregano, and turmeric. I prefer the Goya brand, but it is very easy to make your own.

SHANE'S TOP TIPS

While a number of the tips included in this volume are recipe-specific, the following are good to keep in mind whenever you're in the kitchen:

- Using fresh and whole spices makes all the difference when it comes to flavor. If your dry spices have been in the cabinet for more than a year, chances are they have lost their potency and need to be replaced. Stock up on whole spices and invest in a small spice grinder or an electric coffee grinder to ensure that you always have fresh spices on hand.

- Cooking the perfect chicken can be tricky. If your ideal bird proves continually evasive, try the spatchcocking method, which will ensure that it cooks evenly and that the skin gets crispy. To spatchcock a chicken, place it breast down on a work surface. Take kitchen shears or a knife and cut along the backbone on both sides from top to bottom. Flip the chicken over so that it is breast side up and press down until it lays flat.

- When sautéing, it's important to have the oil at exactly the right temperature. If you want to see if the oil is ready, flick a few drops of water into it. If the oil sizzles, it is warm enough.

- Pearl and cipollini onions are delicious, but preparing them can be a pain since they can be difficult to peel. If you're looking for a way to cut down on your prep time, submerge the onions in boiling water for a few minutes to loosen the skins. Then remove the tops and bottoms with a small knife and squeeze the onions out.

- If you're struggling to peel ginger with a knife or peeler, try using a spoon. This is a trick I learned while working in restaurants and it will save you plenty of time and frustration.

- To accurately gauge the temperature of a chicken, insert a kitchen thermometer at the thickest point, next to the bone. To calibrate the thermometer, submerge the tip in a cup of ice water. It should read 32°F.

- Fish sauce has been gaining in popularity over the past several years, and for good reason: its ability to add umami flavor to a dish is unmatched. But be careful not to overdo it. A good rule of thumb: add just enough fish sauce that you can vaguely smell it.

- For a 1-inch thick steak, 2 minutes on each side should get you to a perfect rare to medium rare.

- For a simple, tasty tomato sauce, combine a 28 oz. can of pureed San Marzano tomatoes, 1 teaspoon of sea salt, and 2 tablespoons of extra virgin olive oil.

- When a recipe calls for seasoned bread crumbs, it's worth taking the time to make your own, since you can control the amount of seasoning. Take half of a baguette (or any crusty or slightly stale bread), add it to a food processor, and process until it has been broken down into fine crumbs. Add 2 tablespoons of extra virgin olive oil and 1 tablespoon each (or to taste) of dried oregano, dried basil, salt, and pepper and pulse until combined.

- To make a balsamic glaze in your home, bring 1 cup of balsamic vinegar to a boil in a small saucepan, reduce the heat, and let it simmer for 10 to 15 minutes. It is ready when it is thick enough to coat the back of a spoon and has the consistency of melted chocolate. Remove from heat, let it cool, transfer to a jar or a squeeze bottle, and store in your refrigerator.

- You can buy roasted garlic, but if you want to do it at home, remove the top of one head of garlic just enough to see the cloves inside their skins, preheat the oven to 375°F, and place the head of garlic, cut-side up, in a square of aluminum foil. Drizzle the garlic with olive oil, place a pat of butter on top, and close the foil over the garlic. Place in the oven and roast for 45 minutes to 1 hour. The garlic cloves should look slightly brown, be extremely fragrant, and be easy to squeeze from their skins.

- If you're like me and you're a stickler for using dried beans instead of canned, don't discard the cooking liquid when you drain the beans after they have cooked. It's great when you want to thicken soups, sauces, and stews.

- When blending hot liquids, remember to leave the top of the blender open slightly so that the pressure inside doesn't build up and send hot sauce over everything! I usually leave the top vent on my blender open and cover the opening with a towel to allow steam to escape.

- When adding alcohol to hot pans, make sure you pull them away from heat before adding the alcohol. This will help you avoid potential fires and injuries.

METRIC CONVERSION CHART

U.S. Measurement	Approximate Metric Liquid Measurement	Approximate Metric Dry Measurement
1 teaspoon	5 mL	—
1 tablespoon or $^1/_2$ ounce	15 mL	14 g
1 ounce or $^1/_8$ cup	30 mL	29 g
$^1/_4$ cup or 2 ounces	60 mL	57 g
$^1/_3$ cup	80 mL	—
$^1/_2$ cup or 4 ounces	120 mL	$^1/_4$ pound / 113 g
$^2/_3$ cup	160 mL	—
$^3/_4$ cup or 6 ounces	180 mL	—
1 cup or 8 ounces or $^1/_2$ pint	240 mL	$^1/_2$ pound / 227 g
1 $^1/_2$ cups or 12 ounces	350 mL	—
2 cups or 1 pint or 16 ounces	475 mL	1 pound / 454 g
3 cups or 1 $^1/_2$ pints	700 mL	—
4 cups or 2 pints or 1 quart	950 mL	—

INDEX

Recipes included in the book are in italics.

ACKNOWLEDGEMENTS

This entire experience has been incredible and exciting. I never thought I'd get the chance to write a cookbook, and I've learned so much from this process.

I'd like to thank Brittany Wason for connecting me with Cider Mill Press. Thanks to Joe and Jill for prepping and testing recipes. To Mel for lending her touch and a few recipes. To Jody and my neighbors for contributing ideas and props. To Johnny for helping with the camera and teaching me so much about photography. To all my friends who came over to try out the food. To my family for being supportive in my endeavor. A huge thanks to publisher John Whalen for taking a chance on me. And endless thanks to Buzz Poole, editors Abigail Brown and Matthew Doucet, designer Mallory Grigg, and everyone at Cider Mill Press for their guidance, patience, and incredible care with this book.

ABOUT THE AUTHOR

Shane Hetherington's journey to the role of executive chef started at the age of 7, when the show *Yan Can Cook* inspired him to pick up a knife and start cooking. Over the course of nearly 20 years in food service, he has become increasingly focused on the flavors available in Mexican and Southwestern cuisine. A food photographer and blogger who is constantly searching for inspiration, Shane also runs a food delivery service where he cooks healthy meals for people on the go.

ABOUT CIDER MILL PRESS
BOOK PUBLISHERS

Good ideas ripen with time. From seed to harvest, Cider Mill Press brings fine reading, information, and entertainment together between the covers of its creatively crafted books. Our Cider Mill bears fruit twice a year, publishing a new crop of titles each spring and fall.

"Where Good Books Are Ready for Press"

Visit us online at
www.cidermillpress.com
or write to us at
PO Box 454
12 Spring St.
Kennebunkport, Maine 04046